PRAYING HYDE

D0789996

PRAYING HYDE

Edited by

Captain E.G. Carré

BRIDGE PUBLISHING, INC. • SOUTH PLAINFIELD, NEW JERSEY

PRAYING HYDE

All rights reserved.
Copyright © 1982 by Bridge Publishing, Inc.
Library of Congress Catalog Card Number: 82-73972
Bridge Publishing, Inc., 2500 Hamilton Boulevard
South Plainfield, New Jersey 07080, USA

ISBN 0-88270-541-5

Printed in the United States of America

Foreword

"THE place where John Hyde met God was holy ground. The scenes of his life are too sacred for common eyes. I shrink from placing them before the public. . . . So we take our stand near the prayer closet of John Hyde, and are permitted to hear the sighing and the groaning, and to see the tears coursing down his face, to see his frame weakened by foodless days and sleepless nights, shaken with sobs as he pleads, 'O God, give me souls or I die!' " In this way, one of the authors of *Praying Hyde,* Francis A. McGaw, introduces us to a mighty prayer warrior and missionary to India, John Hyde.

This little book is a challenge to believers everywhere—a call to intercessory prayer. John Hyde entered a spiritual realm where few men have been, that "place of quiet rest, near to the heart of God." Hyde's story is an invitation into his prayer closet. As you read, you will learn how to be "shut in with God, in the secret place"—and you will desire a deeper life of prayer for yourself.

Few, it would seem, seek to become ministers of intercession. God knows who they are. Through Christian literature we are able to recognize the prayer ministries of men like Andrew Murray, Rees Howells, George Müeller, Evan Roberts and others. In *Praying Hyde* we learn about another man who became a true intercessor and, more importantly, we see the wonderful results of his life of prayer and the principles his life reveals.

As the publishers of this edition, we realize the great need for an awakening of prayer in God's people. Every great revival in history has been preceded by weeks, months—even years—of earnest prayer. It was true of the Great Awakening in America. It was true of the Welsh revival. More recently, it was true of the revivals in Indonesia and Korea. As we go to press with this edition of *Praying Hyde,* our prayer is that it will find its way into the hands of people who will dedicate themselves to intercede for our nation—and our world—so that a heaven-born revival will once again shake the earth.

You are about to meet a man who took his Christian commitment seriously. He was raised in an atmosphere of prayer that became his "native air." As people came in contact with John Hyde—and the presence of God that surrounded him and flowed from him—their lives were changed. As you read, take in that fresh, life-giving breath of God that He gives freely to all who will to be His vessel.

Long ago, God spoke through his prophet, "And I sought for a man among them, that should make up the hedge, and stand in the gap before me for the land, that I should not destroy it: but I found none" (Ezek. 22:30). And one has to wonder where such a man will be found today—an intercessor like John Hyde who will give his life to call our nation back to God. May the Lord use this book to find people who will truly "make up the hedge, and stand in the gap."

—Lloyd B. Hildebrand

Foreword to Third Edition

THE two Indian editions of this remarkable prayer-life having long since been exhausted, it was felt that in order to meet the demand that still continues, the time was ripe for a third issue.

The question then arose as to whether it would be possible to continue the Indian and American publications in one volume, and thus make a standard life of John Hyde, containing full details of his family history, his college days, and his labours on the mission field.

With M'Cheyne Paterson's hearty cooperation, and the gracious consent of the author of the American edition, F. A. M'Gaw, together with the generous permission of the Bible Institute Colportage Association of Chicago, the holders of the American copyright, whose courtesy we gratefully acknowledge, the way has been completely cleared for the present volume to embody the two previous publications in one.

With the exception of the necessary omission of certain matter in order to avoid repetition, and the inclusion of some additional details which have come to hand since the previous edition, Mr. Hyde's life story goes forth in practically the same form in which it was originally issued in the land of his birth, and in that of his labours, and in which it has been so signally blessed to the Church at large. With the prayer that the challenge of such an amazing life of intercession, resulting in such an intimate walk with God, may be mightily used of Him who challenges us to test Him in His promises to the uttermost, we gladly and expectantly commit this unique record to His fatherly care. We have regretfully to mention the death of our friend, J. Pengwern Jones, joint author of the Indian "Life," who passed to his rest some months ago.

E.G.C.

Contents

PART II.

PART III.

PART IV.

CONCLUSION.

Introduction

I HAVE been asked by the Editor to write a few lines of introduction to this little book, and I gladly comply with his request, for, as I have said in the Reminiscences, dear Hyde was made a blessing to me. I had read that precious book by Andrew Murray: "With Christ in the School of Prayer," and in Mr. Hyde I saw a living example of one who actually lived with Christ in the School of Prayer, and his example gave me a deep longing and even an inspiration to be a pupil in this school also.

I was asked by many to write a few Reminiscences of Hyde, and over and over again I purposed doing it, but I believe the time had not come, the Church was not ready for such a record, and probably the Spirit of God saw that I was not ready to write sympathetically such incidents that I wanted to write; but when the Lord began to pour His Spirit upon the Eastern Coast of England and the North of Scotland, and the people of God began to pray more earnestly for a general Revival all over the world, I found no difficulty in writing about dear Hyde's prayer-life, and the account written by his beloved friend, R. M'Cheyne Paterson, was kindly placed at my disposal at that time, and became a further inspiration to me.

The last month or-so I have heard that others have valuable information about Hyde during his college days, probably these incidents in his life will be published as a supplement

I hope that this book will lead many to become "companions" of our Great High Priest. He wants "companions," "fellows," "partakers," to enter with Him into the sanctuary as intercessors. The High Priest of old had to enter into the Holy of Holies *alone*, but our High Priest begs for partners to be with Him. This is what Hyde really was, and it is strange that we should be so reluctant to take up this great privilege of being fellow-intercessors with Him.

I trust that one of the results of reading this book will be the enlistment of many and better intercessors.

I feel grateful to the Editor for undertaking this work, and for the sympathetic and efficient way in which he has carried it through.

May all the glory be unto Him.

J. PENGWERN JONES.

Praying Hyde

PART I

By Francis A. McGaw

PRAYING HYDE

PART I

Christ in the Home

JOHN HYDE, "The Apostle of Prayer," as he was often called, was reared in a home where Jesus was an abiding guest, and where the dwellers in that home breathed *an atmosphere of prayer*. I was well acquainted with John's father, Smith Harris Hyde, D.D., during the seventeen years he was pastor of the Presbyterian Church at Carthage, Illinois. Dr. Herrick Johnson, of Chicago, shortly before he died, wrote these words: "Hyde's father was of rare proportion and balance, a healthful soul, genial and virile, firm of conviction, of good scholarly attainment, of abundant cheer, and bent on doing for God to the best of his ability."

Personally I knew him in his home to be a courteous, loving husband. I knew him to be a firm, yet sympathetic father, commanding his household after him. I knew the sweet-spirited, gentle, music-loving, Christ-like Mrs. Hyde. I knew each one of the three boys and three girls who grew up in that home. Often I have eaten at their table. Twice I have been with the family when the crepe was on the door; once when Mrs. Hyde was taken away, and again when dear John's body was brought home and lovingly laid to rest in Moss Ridge Cemetery. Often I have kneeled with them, and have, as a young minister, been strangely moved when dear Dr. Hyde poured out his heart to God as he prayed at the family altar. I knew him in his church and in the Presbyterial meetings. He was a noble man of God. Under God, his congregation was built up, and he was a leader among his ministerial brethren. I have frequently heard Dr. Hyde pray the Lord of the harvest to thrust out labourers into His harvest. He would pray this prayer both at the family altar and from his pulpit. It is therefore no strange thing that God called two of his sons into the Gospel ministry, and one of his daughters for a time into active Christian work. Dr. Hyde magnified his office, and rejoiced to give his sons up to a life of hardship and trial.

I read in "Far North in India" the statement by a former missionary in India, Dr. W. B. Anderson, that a hundred million people in India to-day have not heard of Jesus Christ, and as things are now have not the remotest chance to hear about Him. There are other millions in Africa and other countries in the same Christless ignorance. Why is it so?

Because prayer closets are deserted, family altars are broken down, and pulpit prayers are formal and dead!

Bible schools and seminaries can never supply the workers needed. My own sainted mother prayed as a young girl that the doors of the heathen countries might be opened. Afterwards as the mother of ten children (eight of whom grew to manhood and womanhood), she prayed for labourers to enter these open doors, and God sent one of her sons to India and two of her daughters to China.

Grandmother Lois and mother Eunice prayed, and when the Great Apostle to the Gentiles was about to take his departure he could lay his hands on son Timothy and commission him to "Preach the Word!"

John Hyde was an answer to prayer, and when in other years he prayed in India, God raised up scores of native workers in answer to his prayers. The Great Head of the Church has provided one method for securing labourers. He said:

"Look on the fields . . . they are white . . . the labourers are few . . . PRAY!"

Holy Ground

In the Tabernacle of Moses there was one room so sacred that only one man of all the thousands of Israel was ever permitted to enter it; and he on one day only of all the three hundred and sixty-five days of the year. That room was the Holy of Holies. The place where John Hyde met God was holy ground. The scenes of his life are too sacred for common eyes. I shrink from placing them before the public.

But when I remember Jacob at the brook, Elijah on Carmel, Paul in his agony for Israel, and especially the Man in the Garden, then I am impressed by the Spirit of God that the experiences of this "Man of God" should be published for the learning and admonition of thousands. So we take our stand near the prayer closet of John Hyde, and are permitted to hear the sighing and the groaning, and to see the tears coursing down his face, to see his frame weakened by foodless days and sleepless nights, shaken with sobs as he pleads, "O God, give me souls or I die!"

Hyde's College Days

Some of his class-mates in the M'Cormick Seminary have kindly lifted up the curtain and allowed us to see something of the spirit which possessed the students of that Seminary during the year 1892, when John Hyde was one of the students. Dr. Herrick Johnson called that class "The Missionary Class of M'Cormick Seminary." Hyde's beloved friend and fellow student—Burton A. Konkle—says: "Out of forty-six students in that class twenty-six decided for the foreign field. Hyde of India was our 'man of prayer.' Lee of Korea has been called 'The Apostle of Korea.' Foster our 'man of suffering,' whose beautiful life influenced us all. They were more to me than my own brother, and I never think of them but with a glow of thankfulness!"

J. F. Young, once Pastor at Hyde's home, said: "I think Konkle is right when he says that Hyde made little impression on any of us (his fellow students), the first year in the seminary, and I rather doubt whether he did the second—he was just one of us, and we did not think much about him. It was during the senior year after the death of his brother Edmund—his eldest brother who was in the Seminary and was a student volunteer for the foreign field—that his fellow-students realised that he was not an ordinary young man. Hyde was greatly impressed by his brother's death, and a great struggle took place as to where his life should be lived. At last he surrendered, and in substance said: "I'll go where you want me to go, dear Lord." The result was a change in his own life, and we began to count it a pleasure to go for a walk with him.

His friend, Mr. Konkle, describes him thus: "During the senior year, when there was a growing interest in foreign missions in our class, Hyde came to my room about eleven o'clock one night and said he wanted all the 'arguments' I had for the foreign field. We sat then for some moments in silence, and then I told him that he knew as much about the foreign field as I did; that I didn't believe it was 'argument' that he needed, and that I thought the way for him to settle it was to lay it before our Father and stay until He decided for him. We sat in silence a while longer, and, saying he believed I was right, he rose and bade me good night. The next morning as I was going up the chapel steps, I felt a hand on my arm, and looking back I saw John's face radiant with a new vision. 'It's settled, Konkle,' said he, and I didn't need to be told how. From that day he grew in power rapidly until, I think we would all agree, he was easily the most powerful single instrument for the foreign field in the Seminary. He prayed for men individually, and then sought them out, and his soul seemed aflame. Prayer was his pathway to greater things, and it became the characteristic of his whole life and work, because it was his peculiar power. He was a torch of prayer, that carried light and warmth. We are only beginning to appreciate the beauty and glory of his life.

"One can see, therefore, how the choice of a field would be to him a mere incident compared to steps in progress, in insight into the Truth, and consequent increased consecration. During that senior year, as organiser of missions, I had appointed him Librarian of the Home Mission Committee, to which field he had, up to that time, seemed most inclined. After he had decided for foreign work, he became restive at giving his time to the home field so much, and came to me asking if I didn't think he should be relieved from it. He knew I was pledged to the foreign field, and yet was organiser of our whole city mission work. So I looked at him with a twinkle in my eye, and asked him if he thought I should be relieved of my work for city missions. He coloured a little, smiled with acquiescence, and said, 'I knew you would say that.' He saw that our principle, *The field is the world*, was one which we could not weaken in our Seminary outlook at least.

"One of our class-mates has spent over thirty years in Korea, and built up sixty-seven churches, and his decision to go abroad was due to Hyde's influence as an instrument."

First Years in India

At the first John Hyde was not a remarkable missionary. He was slow of speech. When a question or a remark was directed to him he seemed not to hear, or if he heard he seemed a long time in framing a reply. His hearing was slightly defective, and this it was feared would hinder him in acquiring the language. His disposition was gentle and quiet; he seemed to be lacking in the enthusiasm and zeal which a young missionary should have. He had a wonderful pair of blue eyes. They seemed to search into the very depth of your inmost being, and they seemed almost to shine out of the soui of a prophet.

On arriving in India, he was assigned the usual language study. At first he went to work on this, but later neglected it for Bible study. He was reprimanded by the committee, but he replied: "First things first." He argued that he had come to India to teach the Bible, and he needed to know it before he could teach it. And God by His Spirit wonderfully opened up the Scriptures to him. Nor did he neglect language study. "He became a correct and easy speaker in Urdu, Punjabi, and English; but away and above that, he learned the language of Heaven, and he so learned to speak that he held audiences of hundreds of Indians spellbound while he opened to them the truths of God's Word."

The Punjab Prayer Union

In every revival there is a Divine side and a human side. In the Welsh revival the Divine element comes out prominently. Evan Roberts, the leader, under God, seems in a sense to have been a passive agent, mightily moved upon in the night seasons by the Holy Spirit. There was no organisation and very little preaching—comparatively little of the human element. The Sialkot revival, while just as certainly sent down from Heaven, seems not so spontaneous. There was, under God, organisation; there was a certain amount of definite planning, and there were seasons of long continued prayer.

Just here, as showing where the human agency avails I wish to mention the *Punjab Prayer Union.* This was started about the time (1904) of the first Sialkot Convention. The principles of this Union are stated in the form of questions which were signed by those becoming members.

1. "Are you praying for quickening in your own life, in the life of your fellow-workers, and in the Church?"

2. "Are you longing for greater power of the Holy Spirit in your own life and work, and are you convinced that you cannot go on without this power?"

3. "Will you pray that you may not be ashamed of Jesus?"

4. "Do you believe that prayer is the great means for securing this spiritual awakening?"

5. "Will you set apart one half-hour each day as soon after noon as possible to pray for this awakening, and are you willing to pray *till the awakening comes*?"

John Hyde was associated with this Prayer Union from its beginning, and also had a definite part in the Sialkot Convention. The members of the Prayer Union lifted up their eyes according to Christ's command and saw the fields—*white to the harvest.* In the Book they read the immutable promises of God.

They saw one method of obtaining this spiritual awakening, even by prayer. They set themselves deliberately, definitely, and desperately to use the means till they secured the result. The Sialkot revival was not an accident nor an unsought breeze from Heaven. Charles G. Finney says: "A revival is no more a miracle than a crop of wheat." In any community revival can be secured from Heaven when heroic souls enter the conflict determined to win or die—or if need be to win and die—"The kingdom of Heaven suffereth violence, and the violent take it by force" (Matt. 11. 12).

Three Men

David's mighty men are catalogued in the Scriptures; there were the first three, then the second three, and afterwards the thirty; Jesus had many unnamed disciples. He had the Twelve, but in the inner circle nearest to himself were the special three: Peter, James, and John. Hundreds came to Sialkot and helped mightily by prayer and praise. But God honoured a few men as leaders. This sketch is not given to flattery or fulsome praise, but God's Word says: "Honour to whom honour is due." God laid a great burden of prayer upon the hearts of John N. Hyde, R. M'Cheyne Paterson, and George Turner for this wonderful convention. There was need for a yearly meeting for Bible Study and prayer, where the spiritual life of the workers—pastors, teachers, and evangelists, both foreign and native—could be deepened. The church life in the Punjab (as indeed in all India), was far below the Bible standard; the Holy Spirit was so little honoured in these ministries that few were being saved from among the Christless millions. Sialkot was the place selected for this meeting, and 1904 became memorable as the date of the First Sialkot Convention.

Before one of the first conventions, Hyde and Paterson waited and tarried one whole month before the opening date. **For thirty days and thirty nights these godly men waited before God in prayer.** Do we wonder that there was power in the convention? Turner joined them after nine days, so that for twenty-one days and twenty-one nights these three men prayed and praised God for a mighty outpouring of His power. Three human hearts that beat as one and that one the heart of Christ, yearning, pleading, crying, and agonising over the Church of India and the myriads of lost souls. Three renewed human wills that by faith linked themselves as with hooks of steel to the omnipotent will of God. Three pairs of fire-touched lips that out of believing hearts shouted, "It shall be done!"

Do you who read these words look at those long-continued vigils, those days of fasting and prayer, those nights of wakeful watching and intercessions, and do you say, "What a price to pay!" Then I point you to scores and hundreds of workers quickened and fitted for the service of Christ; I point you to literally thousands prayed into the kingdom and I say unto you, "Behold, the purchase of such a price!"

Surely Calvary represents a fearful price. But your soul and mine, and the millions thus far redeemed and other millions which may yet be redeemed, a wrecked earth restored back to Eden perfection, the kingdoms of this world wrested from the grasp of the usurper and delivered over to the reign of their rightful King!—when we shall see all this shall we not gladly say, "Behold the purchase"?

1904—The First Sialkot Convention

One of his dearest friends in India writes about the great change that came to John Hyde's spiritual life at this convention in 1904. He writes that though John was a missionary and a child of God, for he had been born of God, he was yet a babe in Christ. He had never been compelled to tarry at his Jerusalem till he was endued with power from on high. But God in his love spoke to him and showed him his great need. At this convention, while he was speaking to his brother missionaries on the work of the Holy Spirit, God spoke to his own soul and opened up to him the Divine plan of sanctification by faith. Such a touch of God, such a light from Heaven, came to him, that he said at the close of the convention: "I must not lose this vision." And he never did lose it, but rather obtained grace for grace, and the vision brightened as he went obediently forward.

Another missionary tells how John came to this convention to lead the Bible studies. During those days he spoke of the length and breadth and height and depth of the love of God. That mighty love seemed to reach out through him and grip the hearts of men and women and draw them closer to God. This brother writes:

"One night he came into my study about half-past nine, and began to talk to me about the value of public testimony. We had an earnest discussion until long after midnight, and I think until after one o'clock, and as I remember it, quite an interesting argument.

"We had asked him on the next evening to lead a meeting for men which was being held in the tabernacle out on the compound, while the women of the convention were holding a meeting of their own in the missionary bungalow.

"When the time for the meeting arrived the men of us were seated there on the mats in the tent, but Mr. Hyde the leader had not arrived. We began to sing, and sang several hymns before he did come in, quite late.

"I remember how he sat down on the mat in front of us, and silent for a considerable time after the singing stopped. Then he arose, and said to us very quietly, 'Brothers, I did not sleep any last night, and I have not eaten anything to-day. I have been having a great controversy with God. I feel that He has wanted me to come here and testify to you concerning some things that He has done for me, and I have been arguing with him that I should not do this. Only this evening a little while ago have I got peace concerning the matter and have I agreed to obey Him, and now I have come to tell you just some things that He has done for me.

"After making this brief statement, he told us very quietly and simply some of the desperate conflicts that he had had with sin, and how God had given him victory. I think he did not talk more than fifteen or twenty minutes, and then sat down and bowed his head for a few minutes, and then said, 'Let us have a season of prayer.' I remember how the little company prostrated themselves upon the mats on their faces in the Oriental manner, and then how for a long time, how long I do not know, man after man rose to his feet to pray, how there was such confession of sin as most of us had never heard before, and such crying out to God for mercy and help.

"It was very late that night when the little gathering broke up, and some of us know definitely of several lives that were wholly transformed through the influence of that meeting."

Evidently that one message opened the doors of men's hearts for the incoming of the great revival in the Indian Church.

1905 Convention— "Brokenheartedness for Sin"

In the spring of each year the Punjab Prayer Union holds its annual meeting. But as preparation for this meeting the leaders spend much time in prayers and fastings and all-night watching. Then when the Union comes together we look to God for guidance during the coming year. "Early in 1905, at that annual meeting, God laid on our hearts," writes a brother, "the burden of a world plunged in sin. We were permitted to share to some extent in the sufferings of Christ. It was a glorious preparation for the Convention in the fall of 1905."

At this convention John Hyde was constantly in the prayer room day and night; he lived there as on the Mount of Transfiguration. The words were burned into his brain as a command from God: "I have set watchmen upon thy walls, O Jerusalem, which shall never hold their peace day or night: ye that are the Lord's remembrancers, take ye no rest and give Him no rest till He establish, and till He make Jerusalem a praise in the earth" (Isa. 62. 6, 7).

There can be no doubt that he was sustained by Divine strength, for are we not told to "endure hardness according to the power of God"—not in our own weakness, but in His strength? It was not the quantity but the quality of sweet childlike sleep that our Father gave His servant which enabled him to continue so long watching unto prayer. One could see from his face that it was the presence of Christ Himself that strengthened his weak body. John Hyde was the principal speaker, but it was from communion with God that he derived his power.

His prayer life was one of absolute obedience to God. I remember once the lunch bell sounded when we were in the prayer room. I heard him whisper: "Father, is it Thy will that I go?" There was a pause, the answer came, he said: "Thank you, Father," and rose with a smile and went to lunch. Needless to say, he recognised his Lord as seated at the table with them, and oh! how many hungry souls were refreshed by his talks.

He was leader of the morning Bible readings, his subject being John 15. 26, 27: "He shall bear witness of Me, and ye also shall bear witness of Me." "Is the Holy Spirit first in your pulpits, pastors?" Do you consciously put Him in front and keep yourselves behind Him when preaching? Teachers, when you are asked hard questions, do you ask His aid as a witness of all Christ's life? He alone was a witness of the incarnation, the miracles, the death, and the resurrection of Christ. So He is the only witness!"

It was a heart-searching message, and many were bowed down under the convicting power. The next morning Mr. Hyde was not allowed to give any further teaching. The chairman came down from his seat and declared the meeting to be in the hands of God's Spirit. How wonderfully He witnessed of Christ and His power to cleanse all who repent. The next morning once again His servant said that he had no fresh message from God. It was pointed out that God would not be mocked—till we had all learned this lesson as to putting the Holy Spirit first at all times God would not give any fresh message. Who can forget that day? How wonderfully those prayers were answered! The watchmen that night in the prayer room were filled with joy unspeakable, and they ushered in the dawn with shouts of triumph. And why not, for we are "more than conquerors through Him who loves us."

At one time John Hyde was told to do something and he went and obeyed, but returned to the prayer room weeping, confessing that he had obeyed God unwillingly. "Pray for me, brethren, that I may do this joyfully." We soon learned after he went out that he had been led to obey triumphantly. Then he received the promise that he would be the (spiritual) father of many children—an Abraham indeed. He entered the hall with great joy, and as he came before the people, after having obeyed God, he spoke three words in Urdu and three in English, repeating them three times: "*Ai Asmani Bak,*" "O Heavenly Father." What followed who can describe? It was as if a great ocean came sweeping into that assembly, and "suddenly there came a sound from Heaven as of a rushing mighty wind, and it filled all the house where they were sitting." Hearts were bowed before that Divine presence as the trees of the wood before a mighty tempest. It was the ocean of God's love being outpoured through one man's obedience. Hearts were broken before it. There were confessions of sins with tears that were soon changed to joy and then to shouts of rejoicing. Truly, we were filled with new wine—the new wine of Heaven!

Here is the experience of one missionary: "Hours alone with God, with no one to see or hear but God were customary; but the fellowship of others in prayer or praise, for *hours*, could it be downright real? On entering the room the problem was solved. At once you knew you were in the holy presence of God, where there could be only awful reality. Others in the room were forgotten except when the combined prayers and praises made you realise the strength and power and sympathy of such fellowship. The hours of waiting on God in communion with others were precious times, when together we waited on God to search us and to speak to us, together interceded for others, together praised Him for Himself and for His wonder-working power. There was a breadth and freedom during those ten days that I never imagined existed on earth. Surely it was for freedom such as this that Christ has set us free. Each one did exactly as he or she felt led to do. Some went to bed early, some prayed for hours, some prayed all night long, some went to the meetings and some to the prayer room, and some to their own rooms, some prayed, some praised, some sat to pray, some kneeled, some lay prostrate on their faces before God, just as the Spirit of God bade them. There was no criticism, no judging of what was being done or said. Each one realised that all superficialities were put away, and that each one was in the awful presence of the Holy God."

The same missionary referred to John Hyde when she wrote: "There were some who knew that God had chosen and ordained them to be 'watchmen.' There were some who had lived for long so near Jehovah that they heard His voice and received orders direct from Him about everything, even as to when they were to watch and pray, and when they were to sleep. Some watched all night long for nights, because God told them to do so, and He kept sleep from them that they might have the privilege and honour of watching with Him over the affairs of His kingdom."

1906—The Lamb on His Throne.

Again at this Convention in answer to prayer God poured out on us by His Spirit a burden for lost souls. We saw the same broken-heartedness for the sins of others. None felt this more than John Hyde. God was deepening his prayer-life. He was permitted of God to have the privilege of drinking of the Master's cup, and of being baptised with His baptism—the second baptism of fire, suffering with Him that we may reign with Him here and now, the life of true kings for the sake of others.

About this time John Hyde began to have visions of the glorified Christ as a Lamb on His Throne—suffering such infinite pain for and with His suffering body on earth, as is so often revealed in God's Word. As the Divine Head, He is the nerve-centre of all the body. He is indeed living to-day a life of intercession for us. Prayer for others is as it were the very breath of our Lord's life in Heaven. "He ever liveth to make intercession for us." It was becoming increasingly true of John Hyde. How often in the prayer room he would break out into tears over the sins of the world, and especially of God's children. Even then his tears would be changed into shouts of praise according to the Divine promise repeated by our Lord on that last night when He talked with His own. "Ye shall be sorrowful, but your sorrow shall be turned into joy" (John 16. 20-22).

A brother writes about the Convention of 1906: "Thank God, He has heard our prayers and poured out the Spirit of grace and intercession upon so many of His children. For example, I saw a Punjabi brother convulsed and sobbing as if his heart would break. I went up to him and put my arms about him, and said, 'The Blood of Jesus Christ cleanseth us from all sin.' A smile lit up his face. 'Thank God, Sahib,' he cried; 'but, oh! what an awful vision I have had! Thousands of souls in this land of India being carried away by the dark river of sin! They are in Hell now! Oh, to snatch them from the fire before it is too late!'"

See another example of how this agony of soul in John Hyde was reflected in one who was a daughter in Christ to him. An Indian Christian girl was at this Convention. Her father had compelled her to neglect Christ's claims upon her. In the prayer room she was convicted of her sin, and told how her heart was being torn away from her father to Christ. One could almost see the springing tendrils of her heart as the power of the love of Christ came upon her. It was a terrible time. Then she asked us to pray for her father. We began to pray, and suddenly the great burden of that soul was cast upon us, and the room was filled with sobs and cries for one whom most of us had never seen or heard of before. Strong men lay on the ground groaning in agony for that soul. There was not a dry eye in that place until at last God gave us the assurance that prayer had been heard and out of Gethsemane we came into the Pentecostal joy of being able to praise Him that He heard our cry.

"That meeting was one," writes this brother, "that will never leave my memory. It went on all night. It was a time when God's power was felt as I never had felt it before."

This brother continues: "God wants those who are willing to bear the burden of the souls of these millions without God, to go with Jesus into Gethsemane. He wants us to do this. It is a blessed experience to feel that in some measure we can enter into the fellowship of Christ's sufferings. It brings us into a precious nearness to the Son of God. And not only this, but it is God's appointed way of bringing the lost sheep back to the fold. He is saying, 'Who will go for us, and whom shall I send?' Are you who read these words willing to be intercessors? If we are willing to put ourselves into God's hands, then God is willing to use us. But there are two conditions: obedience and purity. Obedience in everything, even in the *least*, surrendering up our wills and taking the will of God. And the next step is purity. God wants pure vessels for his service, clean channels through which to pour forth His grace. He wants purity in the very centre of the soul, and unless God can have a pure vessel, purified by the fire of the Holy Spirit, He cannot use that vessel. He is asking you now if you will let Him cleanse away part of your very life. God must have a vessel He can use.

1907—Holy Laughter

In the summer of 1907 John went to a friend's house for a holiday. It was in the M—— Hills. The friend writes about it thus: "The crowning act of God's love to us personally was the wonderful way in which He brought Mr. Hyde up to stay with us. I also had to come up to do duty among some English troops here. So Hyde and I have been having glorious times together. There were seasons of great conflict, and at times I thought Hyde would break down completely. But after all-nights of prayer and praise he would appear fresh and smiling in the morning. God has been teaching us wonderful lessons when He calls us to seasons of such wrestling. It is that command in 2 Timothy 1. 8, 'Suffer hardship with the Gospel *according to the power of God.*' So that we have the power of God to draw upon for all our need. Ever since Mr. Hyde realised this he says he has scarcely ever felt tired, though he has had at times little sleep for weeks. No man need ever break down through overstrain in this ministry of intercession.

"Another element of power: 'The joy of the Lord is your strength.' Ah G——, a poor Punjabi brother of low caste origin, has been used of God to teach us all how to make such times of prayer a very Heaven upon earth, how to prevent the pleasure of praying, and even of wrestling, ever descending into a toil. How often has G——, after most awful crying seemed to break through the hosts of evil and soar up into the presence of the Father! You could see the smile of God reflected in his face. Then he would laugh aloud in the midst of his prayer. It was the joy of a son revelling in the delight of his father's smile. God has been teaching John and me that his name is the God of Isaac—laughter. Have you observed that picture of Heaven in Proverbs 8. 30? 'I was daily His delight.' This is the Father's love being showered upon His own Son. No wonder that in such a home the Son should say that He was 'always rejoicing before Him.' Rejoicing, laughing, the same word as Isaac. This holy laughter seemed to relieve the tension and give Heaven's own refreshment to wrestling spirits.

"I must tell you of dear Hyde's last message before he returned to Ludhiana. It was a special revelation to Paul, and one which the Spirit forced him to give out to the Romans, that he had unceasing pain, for he could wish that he himself were *anathema* from Christ for his kinsmen according to the flesh (Rom. 9. 1-3). Surely this was more than Paul's love for Christ. When he could wish that he should be what Christ had become for us—a curse! Fancy having to give up all hope in Christ! Fancy going back to the old sins and their domination over us! The thought is unbearable! Yet such was the Divine pity in Paul's heart that he was willing to be *anathema* from Christ, if it were possible in this way to save his kinsmen the Jews. Such in a few words was God's message by His messenger, John Hyde. How we all broke down! Ah, God's love was indeed shed abroad in the hearts of those present. All this was leading to the great crisis in John Hyde's prayer-life, which I had the privilege of seeing."

Summer, 1908

"This summer we persuaded him to come up to the hills with us. His room was a separate one upon the hill and to one side of our house. Here he came, but came for a very real intercession with his Master. This intercession was fraught with mighty issues for the kingdom of God amongst us. It was evident to all that he was bowed down with sore travail of soul. He missed many meals, and when I went to his room I would find him lying as in great agony, or walking up and down as if an inward fire were burning in his bones. And so there was that fire of which our Lord spoke when He said: 'I came to cast fire upon the earth, and how would I that it were already kindled! But I have a baptism to be baptised with, and how I am straitened till it be accomplished.' John did not fast in the ordinary sense of the word, yet often at that time when I begged him to come for a meal he would look at me and smile, and say, 'I am not hungry.' No, there was a far greater hunger eating up his very soul, and prayer alone could satisfy that. Before the spiritual hunger the physical disappeared. He had heard our Lord's voice saying to him, 'Abide ye here and watch with Me.' So he abode there with his Lord, who gave him the privilege of entering Gethsemane with Himself."

One thought was constantly uppermost in his mind, that our Lord still agonises for souls. Many times he used to quote from the Old and New Testaments, especially as to the privilege of "filling up that which was lacking of the afflictions of Christ." He would speak of the vow made by our Lord devoting a long drawn out travail of soul till all His own were safely folded. "For I say unto you that I shall not drink henceforth of the fruit of the vine till that day, when I drink it new with you in My Father's kingdom." "Saul, Saul, why persecutest thou Me?" These were some of the verses used of God to open his eyes to the fellowship of Christ's sufferings. These were days when the clouds were often pierced and the glorified life that our Lord now leads shone through, revealing many mysteries of travail and pain. It was truly a following of Him who is the Lamb, suffering still *with* us as He once did *for* us on earth, though now Himself on the throne. John Hyde found that He still carries our crosses—the heavy end of our crosses, "for He ever liveth to make intercession for us."

It was into the life of prayer and watching and agonising for others that he was being led step by step. All this time, though he ate little and slept less, he was bright and cheerful. Our children had ever been a great joy to him. Uncle John, who had so often played with them, was always welcomed with smiles of love. Yet now, even the little ones appeared to realise that this was no time for play! They were wonderfully subdued and quiet in his presence in those days, for there was a light on his face that told of communion with another world. Yet there was nothing of the hermit about him—in fact, people were more than ever attracted to him, and freely asked for his prayers. He always had leisure to speak to them of spiritual things, and entered even more patiently than ever into their trials and disappointments. We will not speak in detail of those days of watching and praying and fasting, when he appeared to enter into our Lord's great yearning for His sheep. We feared his poor weak body would sink under the strain; but how marvellously he was sustained all the time! At times that agony was dumb, at times it was a crying out for the millions perishing before our eyes; yet it was always lit up with hope. Hope in the love of God—Hope in the God of love.

With all that depth of love which he seemed to be sounding with his Lord, there were glimpses of its heights—moments of Heaven upon earth, when his soul was flooded with songs of praise, and he would enter into the joy of his Lord. Then he would break into song, but they were always "songs in the night." In those days he never seemed to lose sight of those thousands in his own district without God and without hope in the world. How he pleaded for them with sobs—dry choking sobs, that showed how the depths of his soul were being stirred. "Father, give me these souls, or I die!" was the burden of his prayers. His own prayer that he might rather burn out than rust out was already being answered.

Let me introduce here a gem from the pen of Paterson: "What was the secret of that prayer-life of John Hyde's?" he asks. "This, that it was a life of prayer. Who is the source of all life? The glorified Jesus. How do I get this life from Him? Just as I receive His righteousness to begin with. I own that I have no righteousness of my own—

only filthy rags, and I in faith claim His righteousness. Now, a twofold result follows: As to our Father in Heaven, He sees Christ's righteousness—not my unrighteousness. A second result as to ourselves: Christ's righteousness not merely clothes us outwardly, but enters into our very being, by His Spirit, received in faith as with the disciples (see John. 20. 22), and works out sanctification in us."

Why not the same with our prayer life? Let us remember the word "for." "Christ died for us," and "He ever liveth to make intercession 'for' us," that is, in our room and stead. So I confess my ever-failing prayers (it dare not be called a life), and plead His never failing intercession. Then it affects our Father, for He looks upon Christ's prayer-life in us, and answers accordingly. So that the answer is far "above all we can ask or think." Another great result follows: it affects us. Christ's prayer life enters into us, and He prays in us. This is prayer in the Holy Spirit. Only thus can we pray without ceasing. This is the life more abundant which our Lord gives. Oh, what peace, what comfort! No more working up a life of prayer and failing constantly. Jesus enters the boat, and the toiling ceases, and we are at the land whither we would be. Now, we need to be still before Him, so as to hear His voice and allow Him to pray in us—nay, allow Him to pour into our souls His overflowing life of intercession, which means literally: FACE TO FACE meeting with God—real UNION and COMMUNION.

1908 Convention—One Soul a Day

It was about this time that John Hyde laid hold of God in a very definite covenant. This was for one soul a day—not less, not inquirers simply, but a soul saved—ready to confess Christ in public and be baptised in His Name. Then the stress and strain was relieved. His heart was filled with the peace of full assurance. All who spoke to him perceived a new life and a new life-work which this life can never end.

He returned to his district with this confidence; nor was he disappointed. It meant long journeys, nights of watching unto prayer, and fasting, pain, and conflict, yet victory always crowning this. What though the dews chilled him by night and the drought exhausted him by day? His sheep were being gathered into the fold, and the Good Shepherd was seeing of the travail of his soul and being satisfied. By the end of that year more than four hundred were gathered in.

Was he satisfied? Far from it. How could he possibly be so long as his Lord was not? How could our Lord be satisfied, so long as one single sheep was yet outside His fold? But John Hyde was learning the secret of Divine strength: "The joy of the Lord."

For, after all, the greater our capacity for joy, the greater our capacity also for sorrow. Thus it was with the Man of Sorrows, He who could say: "These words have I spoken unto you, that My joy may be in you and that your joy may be full."

John Hyde seemed always to be hearing the Good Shepherd's voice saying, "Other sheep I have—other sheep I have." No matter if He won the one a day or two a day or four a day, He had an unsatisfied longing, an undying passion for lost souls. Here is a picture given by one of his friends in India: "As a personal worker he would engage a man in a talk about his salvation. By and by he would have his hands on the man's shoulders, looking him very earnestly in the eye. Soon he would get the man on his knees confessing his sins and seeking salvation. Such a one he would baptise in the village, by the roadside, or anywhere.

"I once attended one of his conventions for Christians. He would meet his converts as they came in, and embrace them in Oriental style, laying his hand first on one shoulder and then on the other. Indeed, his embraces were so loving that he got nearly all to give like embraces to Christians, and those, too, of the lowest caste."

This was his strong point. *Love won him victories.*

1909 Convention—Two Souls a Day

Again John Hyde laid hold of God with a definite and importunate request. This time it was for two souls a day. At this Convention God used him even more mightily than ever before. God spoke through His servant John Hyde.

We speak with bated breath of the most sacred lesson of all—glimpses that He gave us into the Divine heart of Christ broken for our sins. He did not overwhelm us with this sight all at once. He revealed these glimpses gently and lovingly according to our ability to endure it. Ah, who can forget how He showed us His great heart of love pierced by that awful sorrow at the wickedness of the whole world, "which grieved Him at His heart!"

Deeper and deeper we were allowed to enter into the agony of God's soul, till like the prophet of sorrow, Jeremiah, we heard His anguish, desiring that his eyes might become a fountain of tears, that he might weep day and night for the slain of the daughter of his people. There the Divine longing was realised in Gethsemane and Calvary! We were led to see the awful suffering of the Son of God, and the still more awful suffering of the Father and of the Eternal Spirit, through whom He offered up Himself without spot unto God.

How can we enter into the fellowship of such sufferings? "Ask, and it shall be given you; seek, and ye shall find; knock, and it shall be opened unto you." Observe the progress in intensified desire—great, greater, greatest, and the corresponding reward till, to crown it all, the Father's heart is thrown open to us. Yes, to all and sundry we tell our joys; it is the privileged few very near our hearts to whom we tell our sorrows. So it is with the love of God. It was to John the Beloved as he lay close to the heart of the Master, and then drew closer still, that Jesus revealed the awful anguish that was breaking His heart, that one of them should betray Him. The closer we draw to His heart, the more we shall share His sorrows. All this we obtain only by faith. It is not our broken heart, it is God's we need. It is not our sufferings, it is Christ's we are partakers of. It is not our tears with which we should admonish night and day, it is all Christ's. The fellowship of His sufferings is His free gift—free for the taking in simple faith, never minding our feelings.

"Lord, give me Thy heart of love for sinners, Thy broken heart for their sins, Thy tears with which to admonish night and day," cried a dear child of God at the end of this Convention. Then he went on:

"But, O Lord, I feel so cold. My heart is so hard and dead. I am so lukewarm!" A friend had to interrupt him. "Why are you looking down at your poor self, brother? Of course your heart is cold and dead. But you have asked for the broken heart of

Jesus, His love, His burden for sin, His tears. Is He a liar? Has He not given what you asked for? Then why look away from His heart to your own?"

John used to say, "When we keep near to Jesus it is He who draws souls to Himself through us, but He must be lifted up in our lives; that is, we must be crucified with Him. It is 'self' in some shape that comes between us and Him, so self must be dealt with as He was dealt with. Self must be *crucified, dead* and *buried* with Christ. If not 'buried,' the stench of the old man will frighten souls away. If *these three steps downwards* are taken as to the old man, then the new man will be *revived, raised, and seated* —the *corresponding steps upward* which God permits us to take. Then indeed Christ is lifted up in our lives, and He cannot fail to attract souls to Himself. All this is the result of a close union and communion that is 'fellowship' with Him in His sufferings!"

1910 Convention—Four Souls a Day

The eight hundred souls gathered in since last year's Convention did not satisfy John Hyde. God was enlarging his heart with His love. Once again he laid hold on God with holy desperation. How many weeks it was I do not remember, but he went deeper still with Christ into the shadows of the Garden! Praying took the form now of confessing the sins of others and taking the place of those sinners, as so many of the prophets did in old time. He was bearing the sins of others alone with his Lord and Master. "Bear ye one another's burdens, and so fulfill the law of Christ." According to that law we ought to lay down our lives for the brethren. This John Hyde was doing. He was "dying daily."

What was that burden referred to in Galatians 6. 2? The previous verse reveals it. It was bearing the sins of others. He at length got the assurance of *four souls a day*!

Yet this was the year that God used him all over India. He was called to help in revivals and conferences in Calcutta, Bombay, and many of the larger cities. Surely he was being prepared for an eternity-wide mission. Yet he was never more misjudged and misunderstood. But that, too, was part of the fellowship of Christ's pain. "He came unto His own, and His own received Him not."

We who were so privileged saw in John Hyde's life the deepening horror of sin during that year of 1910, though it was all but a pale reflection of the awful anguish over sin that at length broke our Saviour's heart. Before this year's Convention he spent long nights in prayer to God. This burden had lain now for five years on his heart—each year pressing heavier and heavier. How it had eaten into his very soul! One saw the long sleepless nights and weary days of watching with prayer written on every feature of his face. Yet his figure was almost transformed as he gave forth God's own words to His people with such fire and such force that many hardly recognised the changed man with the glory of God lighting up every feature. It was Jehovah's messenger speaking Jehovah's message, and we who had shared some of its burden in prayer knew that it was God's own burden *spoken to His Church in India—yes, to His Church throughout the whole world.*

We were transported to Mount Sinai and to the sin of Israel in worshipping the golden calf. Up till that time Moses had not interceded for God's people. Why? Because he had not yet entered into the sufferings of God's heart over sin. So he is sent down among the sinners. *Sin cost him the presence of God.* Was he not being made a partaker of the sufferings of the Lamb slain from the foundation of the world? Then he fasts a second forty days and forty nights (Deut. 9. 19). "For I was afraid of the anger and hot displeasure, wherewith Jehovah was wroth against you to destroy you. But Jehovah hearkened unto me that time also." Moses reports this in 9. 25, doubly emphasised by the Holy Spirit. Surely the Great White Throne in its awful purity shone among us from that time right on through the Convention—no wonder we were filled with shame and confusion of face as were so many of

God's intercessors of old—Moses, Job, Ezra, Nehemiah, Isaiah, Jeremiah, Ezekiel, and Daniel. When God said to Moses, "*Let Me alone,*" He revealed the power of intercession. No! Moses "stood in the breach," and the wrath of God was stayed. He gave up the honour and glory of his own name and family for the sake of God's people. "The Church in the wilderness" was saved by one who shadowed forth our Great Divine Intercessor and partook of His Spirit.

I remember John telling me that in those days if on any day four souls were not brought into the fold, at night there would be such a weight on his heart that it was positively painful, and he could not eat nor sleep. Then in prayer he would ask his Lord to show him what was the obstacle in him to this blessing. He invariably *found that it was the want of praise in his life.* This command, which has been repeated in God's Word hundreds of times—surely it is *all important*! He would then confess his sin, and accept the forgiveness by the Blood. Then he would ask for the spirit of praise as for any other gift of God. So he would exchange his ashes for Christ's garland, his mourning for Christ's oil of joy, his spirit of heaviness for Christ's garment of praise (the Song of the Lamb—praising God beforehand for what He was going to do), and as he praised God souls would come to him, *and the numbers lacking would be made up.*

And now, farewell to Sialkot! As far as this sketch is concerned, we are leaving those hallowed scenes. Others there are who will assemble on those holy grounds; others care for the great company that annually assembles in those audiences; others will keep watch in the prayer room; but as for our dear brother Hyde, 1910 was his last year at Sialkot. We may wonder why it should be so. Only forty-seven, surely his taking away seemed untimely. But God in Heaven knows how wonderfully rounded out were the years of dear John Hyde. Seven Sialkot Conventions, and seven wonderful years of prayer. Surely God saw in John Hyde a well rounded out experience and character. Surely God and the recording angel know that the fruitage will be bountiful at the ingathering at the great harvest home. "He that soweth bountifully shall also reap bountifully."

But before we leave Sialkot I am led to record my appreciation of our brother, M'Cheyne Paterson. "Paterson, I have fallen in love with you in the Lord. Because you loved Hyde, I love you. Often, dear brother, I have prayed for you, and shall yet pray." And will not all who read this sketch join me in praying for the Convention at Sialkot, and for this precious man of God, still praying and preaching and praising there?

Calcutta and the Doctor

John Hyde was only one of many men who have hazarded life for God's service. Nehemiah was warned of the plotting of Sanballat and Tobiah. He was advised to go into the house of God and shut the doors. He answered, "Should such a man as I flee? And who is there that, being such as I, would go into the temple to save his life? *I will not go in.*"

Of Jesus it is written, "And it came to pass, when the days were well-nigh come that He should be received up, He stedfastly set His face to go to Jerusalem" (Luke 9. 51).

When Mr. Moody was in England the last time, he was having trouble with his heart. He was examined by an eminent physician, who told him that his excessive labours were costing him his life. He was killing himself. He promised that he would not work so hard.

On the voyage back to America, an awful storm struck his ship, the *Spree.* She was partly submerged, and in great distress the people appealed to Mr. Moody. He exhorted and prayed. He told the Lord at that time that if He would get them out of this trouble he would never let up in his labours for lost souls.

That summer was the time of the World's Fair in Chicago. Mr. Moody gathered such a band of preachers, evangelists, workers, and singers as probably never was assembled for such work before or since. Hall, storerooms, theatres, churches, and even circus tents were utilised for Gospel meetings, Mr. Moody worked with all his old-time vigour. They "put over" a magnificent campaign. A few months later, at Kansas City, while on the platform preaching with all his tremendous energy, the great evangelist's heart gave way, his voice ceased, and his labours on earth were over. A few days later, among his friends at Northfield, he passed over to join that heroic band who counted not their lives dear unto themselves, that they might win precious souls to Jesus.

A friend of John Hyde's, living in Calcutta, who now knows what it means to be despised and rejected of men, gives the following testimony as to John's prayer life. "I remember W.T. speaking of dear Hyde's having spent thirty days and nights in prayer for the *great* Sialkot Convention (that was in 1906), when the Convention was opened for the first time to all Christians.

"This news made a deep impression on me, as it stood out in such contrast to my own prayerless life at that time. When he and I were alone, I pressed Turner for more details, particulars of which he was very reluctant to give (as he himself had stayed twenty-one days with the little prayer band). I cannot go into details,' he said, 'but it was a time in the Mount with God.'"

Soon after the 1910 Sialkot Convention, John Hyde held a meeting in Calcutta. His friend in that city writes about him: "He stayed with us nearly a fortnight, and during the whole time he had fever. Yet he took the meetings regularly, and how God spoke to us, though he was bodily unfit to do any work! At that time I was unwell for several days. The pain in my chest kept me awake for several nights. It was then that I noticed what Mr. Hyde was doing in his room opposite. The room where I was being in darkness, I could see the flash of the electric light when he got out of bed and turned it on. I watched him do it at twelve, and at two, and at four, and then at five. From that time the light stayed on till sunrise. By this I know that in spite of his night watches and illness, he began his day at five.

"I shall never forget the lessons I learned at that time. I had always claimed exemption from night watches, as I felt too tired at bed-time. Had I ever prayed for the privilege of waiting upon God in the hours of night? No! This led me to claim that privilege then and there. The pain which had kept me awake night after night was turned into joy and praise because of this new ministry which I had suddenly discovered, of keeping watch in the night with the Lord's "Remembrancers." At length the pain quite left my chest, sleep returned, but with it the fear came upon me lest I should miss my hours of communion with God. I prayed, 'Lord, wake me when the hour comes' (see Isa. 50. 4). At first it was at two A.M., and afterwards at four with striking regularity. At five every morning I heard a Mohammedan priest at the Mosque near by call out for prayers in a ringing, melodious voice. The thought that I had been up an hour before him filled me with joy.

"But Mr. Hyde grew worse, and the annual meeting of his Mission was calling him. Being anxious, I induced him to come with me to a doctor. The next morning the doctor said: 'The heart is in an awful condition. I have never come across such a bad case as this. It has been shifted out of its natural position on the left side to a place over on the right side. Through stress and strain it is in such a bad condition that it will require months and months of strictly quiet life to bring it back again to anything like its normal state. What have you been doing with yourself? Unless you change your whole life and give up the strain, you will have to pay the supreme penalty within six months."

This was the doctor's stern warning. Hyde was to give up his life of strain as an intercessor in the Sanctuary, or pay the penalty with his life. What was to be done? He chose the latter without a moment's hesitation.

"Evermore bearing about in my body
The imminence of such a death as Jesus died."
(2 Cor. 4. 10).

If this was Paul's Hymn of Triumph it was dear Hyde's, too. Can I ever forget his radiant face after the doctor had told him the worst?

"They loved not their lives unto the death" (Rev. 12. 11).

After the doctor's examination, we returned home, and I had taken the precaution of asking for a certificate, which I used in defence and explanation of Hyde's absence from the Annual Conference.

Would he write a letter to meet possible misunderstandings? He lifted the blotter on his table and showed me a letter of six pages written to the Missionary Conference containing his annual report. "Let us post it immediately," I urged. "It is not finished," he quietly said. The letter and report was never posted, because it remained unfinished, as the severe pain in his head (due to his weak condition after his nightly fever), prevented him from finishing it.

"It is my cross, shall I not bear it?" he asked me. There is but one answer to such a question. Misjudged by his brethren, misunderstood by the world, superseded in office, but waxing strong in spirit all the while, for whatever is born of God overcometh the world; "and this is the victory that overcometh the world (and every circumstance) even our faith" (1 John 5. 4).

Then the friend writes how God taught him to live a life of prayer through Mr. Hyde's example, and how afterwards he, too, like John Hyde, was led into the fellowship of Christ's sufferings, down, down, down, farther and farther into the very recesses of Gethsemane, till he, too, seemed to tread the wine-press of the wrath of God against sin all alone.

"The spirit jealousy desires us for His own" (James 4. 5, Alford). It is His highest desire that there be in us a life of fellowship with Himself. For this supreme wish of His heart He rises early, seeking, knocking, unasked, uninvited (Isa. 50. 4). How much more if asked and invited! Does not this fact make the morning watch unspeakably precious and glorious?

He seeks communion with us because it is His right and our benefit. He seeks this communion at the beginning of the day. He would claim the best, the very best hours of the day. With so great a privilege pressed upon us, does it not mean a solemn obligation on our part to cultivate this life of fellowship?

If we are willing, He will quicken and empower.

Remember Gethsemane! Our Lord's appeal to His disciples in His hour of supreme crisis was:

"Could ye not watch with Me one hour?" The appeal, though thrice repeated, fell upon deaf ears, because the enemy's power had overmastered the disciples through sleep. Do we not hear the Lamb upon His throne, standing as though He had been slain, make the same appeal again at this hour of world-crisis, at this hour of Church-crisis, "Could ye not watch with Me one hour?" The renewal of the Church will depend on the renewal of our prayer life. The powers of the world to come are at our disposal if we will make time for quiet hours for fellowship and communion, which is our Lord's supreme yearning desire.

The Calcutta friend concludes: "We have heard of martyrs who were kept in prison, and in the end were put to death. But have we ever heard of one who was so given up to the ministry of prayer that the strain of a daily burden brought him to a premature grave?" "No, friend," answers another brother in India, "not a premature grave; it was the grave of Jesus Christ. John Hyde laid down his life calmly and deliberately for the Church of God in India."

"Who follows in his train?"

Transformed Lives

Behold how much was wrought in the life and work of one lady missionary. She had worked hard for many years in her district, and none of the work there was bearing real fruit. She read the account of Mr. Hyde's prayer-life, and resolved to devote the best hours of her time to prayer and waiting on God in the study of His Word and will. She would make prayer primary, and not secondary as she had been doing. She would begin to live a prayer-life in God's strength. God had said to her: "Call upon Me, and I will show thee great and mighty things. You have not called upon Me, and therefore you do not see these things in your work." She writes: "I felt that at any cost I must know Him and this prayer-life, and so at last the battle of my heart was ended and I had the victory." One thing she prayed for was that God would keep her hidden. She had to face being misunderstood and being dumb and not opening her mouth in self-defence if she was to be a follower of the Lamb.

In less than a year she wrote a letter, and oh, what a change! New life everywhere—the wilderness being transformed into a garden. Fifteen were baptised at first, and one hundred and twenty-five adults during the first half of the following year!

"The most of the year has been a battle to keep to my resolution. I have always lived so active a life, accustomed to steady work all day long, and my new life called for much of the best part of the day to be spent in prayer and Bible study. Can you not imagine what it was and what it is sometimes now? To hear others going around hard at work while I stayed quietly in my room, as it were inactive. Many a time I have longed to be out again in active work among the people in the rush of life, but God would not let me go. His hand held me with as real a grip as any human hand, and I knew that I could not go. Only the other day I felt this again and God seemed to say to me, 'What fruit had ye in those things whereof ye are now ashamed?' Yes, I knew I was ashamed of the years of almost prayer-less missionary life.

"Every department of the work now is in a more prosperous condition than I have ever known it to be. The stress and strain have gone out of my life. The joy of feeling that my life is evenly balanced, the life of communion on the one hand and the life of work on the other, brings constant rest and peace. I could not go back to the old life, and God grant that it may always be impossible."

Another year passed, and she wrote again: "The spirit of earnest inquiry is increasing in the villages and there is every promise of a greater movement in the future than we have ever yet had. Our Christians now number six hundred in contrast with one sixth of that number two years ago (before she began the prayer-life and gave herself to it). I believe we may expect soon to see great things in India. Praise for His hourly presence and fellowship!"

The pastor of a congregation in Illinois writes: "We have lost a strong and noble brother, who has not only done the Lord's work in the far-off land, but has been an inspiration to us as well, and the means of awakening at least one from this congregation to such an interest in the foreign work that to-day she is in China." Who can measure John Hyde's influence and power in India, in England, and in America!

"J. N. Hyde was like his father. When duty called, the call was imperative. He answered it not with sky-rocket exploitation and great ado, but with unalterableness of purpose that meant this or death! It seems God meant this and death. In the last class letter he wrote to his seminary classmates, he says: 'For three full years now God has given us decisions and baptisms every day when we have been out in our district—*over a thousand the past two years* . . . never a day, if we were right with God, without souls.' 'They that turn many to righteousness shall shine as the stars for ever and ever.' Is there anything in this old world worth while except seeking and saving that which was lost?" (Herrick Johnson).

Read of these experiences, as recorded by a missionary in India, who wrote:

"An American Girl's Struggle and Surrender.

"On the wall in my room in India hung a motto card. It is the picture of a stony hill with a little green grass here and there. On the top of the hill is a tree; most of the branches on one side have been entirely swept away by the wind, and only a few scraggly limbs remain on the other side. On this card is printed, 'Endure when there is every external reason not to endure.' And this verse, 'He endured . . . seeing Him who is invisible.'

"A dear young friend seeing this card said to me, 'Memsahib, that motto card is to me your photograph. God has been cutting from your life one branch after another, and again and again has removed earthly supports.'"

She and her husband were very happy in their going out to India and during the first year. But there were shadows over the pathway. The next year God gave and soon took to Himself a dear little life. From the first her husband would ask God to fill him with the Spirit at any cost to himself. At first she could not pray this prayer. After the babe was taken she would join her husband in this prayer, and as they would rise from their knees she would say, "But, oh, I am afraid of the cost." Then next her husband was taken with fever. How she pleaded and prayed and even commanded God. But he passed away. For months she was dazed and seemed oblivious to everything but her unutterable loss. It was a year of great darkness.

But in the spring God sent a messenger (Mr. Reginald Studd, a man from whom John Hyde learned much), through whom God revealed what He desired to be to each of His children, their all in all, the chiefest among ten thousand, their heart-friend.

Christ possessed this man's life. Christ was to him all that the dearest earthly friend could be, and infinitely more. Not only was his life centred in Christ—Christ was his very life. He communed with Him as with a friend, spending hours with Him, his inmost being was made radiant with Christ's abiding presence, and wherever he went "Christ was revealed." Soon after meeting this messenger of Christ she relates further: "In a written consecration I gave myself, my child (born shortly after her husband's death), all I had and all I ever would have, to the Lord, to be His for ever. It was an unconditional surrender, and the Holy Spirit entered in His fulness and began to lead me into the love and joy and peace—a knowledge surpassing the love and joy and peace for which I had long been yearning. There came to my heart a deep quietness. The Word of God opened up to me in marvellous richness, becoming food for the soul.

"In the years that have followed I have again and again been brought to places where two ways opened;

one the way of the ordinary Christian life, the other the way on which one seemed to see the blood-stained marks of the Saviour's footsteps; and he called me to follow Him—the slain Lamb. It has meant the way of the Cross; but it has also meant fellowship with Christ."

She writes further about the "Messenger" whom God had sent to the Punjab, who showed such a Christ-possessed life. She writes: "I do not remember that he ever talked about prayer; *he prayed.* Speaking sometimes four and five times a day, he would then spend half the night in prayer, sometimes alone, sometimes with others. He prayed."

She gives us modestly some glimpses of how wonderfully God worked through her. Sometimes it was among the Mohammedans, sometimes among the native Hindus, and sometimes among the foreign missionaries. She was associated with the Punjab Prayer Union and the Sialkot Convention.

She says: "There have been many failures, times when the self-life hindered God. I am more and more amazed that God has been able, notwithstanding my failures, to work in such wondrous ways, and has given me the joy of seeing Him work.

"God offers," she continues, "to bring all who are willing into the secret place, within the veil, the place of sweetest refuge, where 'all is peace and quiet stillness.'"

When I was a boy there was a pond near my father's house. I would stand on the shore of that pond and throw a stone out into the water and then watch the waves in ever widening circles move out from that centre, till every part of the surface of the pond would be in motion. The waves would come to the shore at my very feet, and every little channel and inlet would be moved by the ripples.

Sialkot started circles and waves of blessing that are even now beating in the secret recesses and inlets of many human hearts. And I am led to believe that every atom and molecule of water in that pond felt the impact of that stone. Only God and the recording angel can determine how much the whole body of Christ has been moved upon and benefited by the tremendous prayer force generated by the Holy Spirit in that prayer room at Sialkot.

Native pastors, teachers, and evangelists have gone home from these conventions with new zeal for Jesus Christ, and have influenced thousands of lives in their many fields of labour.

Foreign missionaries have had their lives deepened by visions of God. Letters and printed pages, like the aprons and handkerchiefs from Paul's body, have been sent probably to every country on earth to bring healing to the faint-hearted, and direction and encouragement to those desiring to enter the prayer-life. I am assured that tens of thousands have been born into the kingdom because of the soul travail at Sialkot. Myriads will one day rise up to thank God that two or three men in North India in the name of Jehovah said, "Let us have a convention at Sialkot!"

Home at last

The meeting and visit in Calcutta occurred in the fall or winter following the 1910 Sialkot Convention.

The next spring, March, 1911, John Hyde started home as the physicians would say a "dying man." He had arrived in India in the autumn of 1892, less than twenty years before. But surely they were nineteen beautiful years.

After a stay in England, John Hyde arrived in New York, August 8, 1911. He went at once to Clifton Springs, N.Y. His purpose was to obtain relief from a severe headache, from which he had suffered much before leaving India. A tumour soon developed which when operated on became malignant and was pronounced by the physician to be sarcoma, for which as yet medical science has found no remedy. He rallied from this operation, and on December 19, went to his sister, the wife of Prof. E. H. Mensel, at Northampton, Mass.

But soon after New Year's Day he began to have pains in his back and side. He thought it was rheumatism, but the physician knew it was the dreaded sarcoma again.

He passed away February 17, 1912. His body was taken by his brother Will Hyde, and his sister Mary back to the old home at Carthage, Illinois, and the funeral was held in the church where his father was for seventeen years the pastor. At the time of John's funeral J. F. Young, his classmate was pastor of the home church, and preached at the funeral. It was my privilege to assist in the service and to stand on the platform and look down into the casket at that dear, dear face. He was greatly emaciated, but it was the same sweet, peaceful, gentle yet strong, resolute face that I had known in 1901—the last time I saw him alive.

That February the 20th was cloudy and chill and gloomy as out in beautiful Moss Ridge we tenderly laid him beside his father and his mother and his brother Edmund. But I know that by and by the clouds and the shadows will flee away, the chill and gloom of the grave be dispelled, and that man of prayer and praise come forth in the likeness of the risen Son of God!

Holiness unto the Lord

As I have carefully and prayerfully gone over the facts and incidents and experiences in the life of my dear friend, I am impressed that the one great characteristic of John Hyde was *holiness.* I do not mention prayerfulness now, for prayer was his life work.

I do not especially call attention to soul-winning, for his power as a soul-winner was due to his Christ-likeness. God says, "Without holiness no man shall see the Lord," and we may Scripturally say without holiness no man shall be a great soul-winner. Mr. Hyde himself said in substance, "Self must not only be dead, but buried out of sight, for the stench of the unburied self-life will frighten souls away from Jesus."

It does not seem that John Hyde preached much about his own personal experience of sanctification, but he lived the sanctified life. His life preached. Just as he did not say very much about prayer. He prayed. His life was a witness to the power of Jesus' Blood to cleanse from all sin.

Read these testimonies that have come to me from a number of sources. Further search would no doubt reveal scores of other witnesses to the saintliness of this beloved servant of Jesus Christ and man of prayer.

From a publication in this country: "The Bishop of Oxford says of personal holiness, '*There is no power on the world so irrepressible as the power of personal holiness.*' A man's gifts may lack opportunity, his efforts be misunderstood and resisted, but the spiritual power of a consecrated will needs no opportunity, and can enter where doors are shut. In this strange and tangled business of human life there is no energy that so steadily does its work as the mysterious, unconscious, silent, unobtrusive, impenetrable influence which comes from a man who has done with all self-seeking. And herein lay John Hyde's mystical power and great influence. Multitudes have been brought to their knees by prayer he uttered when filled with the Spirit."

This from a letter written to Mr. Hyde's sister: "If ever there was a godly man, forgetful of himself and devoted to the Master's service, your brother was that one."

A native of India: "The marvellous spirituality of Mr. Hyde had for some time been so great that all who saw it were filled with wonder." These words are by a missionary in India: "His loss will be sadly felt in this country, especially by the Indian Christians. He was one of the holiest men I have ever known, and his life exerted a great influence."

One of his classmates writes: "No saint of the Church was ever beyond him in holiness. He verily gave his life for Christ and India."

Another missionary in India wrote: "He revealed a Christ-possessed prayer-life. He talked with Christ as with a friend, spending hours with Him. His inmost being was made radiant by Christ's abiding presence, and wherever he went Christ was revealed."

The *Indian Witness* says this: "He has had a very remarkable influence in the Indian Church. A year ago last autumn his addresses at the Sialkot Convention produced a profound impression. He was an acceptable speaker in Urdu, Punjabi, and in English, and it was always the man of holiness and power back of an address which made it indeed a message."

Another Indian missionary writes: "He had become a real prophet of God. He was truly one who spoke for God. Thoughtful men would sit for hours during a day listening to his wonderful exposition of truth, as he slowly, quietly, and clearly set forth what the Spirit of God had taught him from His Word."

Not only was his the word of a prophet, but his life had been sanctified by the truth. One day a missionary was talking to a young Hindu who had become acquainted with Mr. Hyde, when the Hindu said, "Do you know, sir, that Mr. Hyde seems to me like God." He was not far from the truth, for in a sense unknown to his Hindu understanding this man had become an Incarnation. I quote from a postal card written by John to his sister while he was at Clifton Springs, N.Y., dated October 27th, 1911, "Am still in bed or wheel-chair, getting a fine rest and doing a lot of the ministry of intercession, and having not a few opportunities of personal work. *How the radiance of Holiness shone out in Jesus' every word and deed!*" Yes, dear heart, and we can truthfully and reverently say, "How the radiance of holiness shone out in John Hyde's every word and deed."

Victory

"The last enemy that shall be destroyed is Death" (1 Cor. 15. 26). John Hyde had faced the enemy too many times in going over into "No Man's Land" to rescue the dying, to be frightened when the last awful encounter took place that February day in 1912. When John Hyde was in England, Mr. Charles M. Alexander took him to his own doctor, and then a consultation with two other physicians was held. The doctor then endeavoured to impress Mr. Hyde with the seriousness of his condition. Mr. Alexander listened to the conversation. Surely Mr. Hyde understood that really he was then in a dying condition. Both Mr. Alexander and the doctor were amazed at Mr. Hyde's perfect composure. He had long ago ceased to fear death, and for him to depart and be with Christ was far better.

I am persuaded that no words of mine could fittingly bring this sketch to a close. But the description I am using is from the pen of Dr. W. B. Anderson in "The Men's Record and Missionary Review" (United Presbyterian). Dr. Anderson was for some years himself a missionary in India, and was chairman of the committee that established the Sialkot Convention. He was well acquainted with dear John Hyde. He writes: "He went a long way into the suffering of India, and he had desperate encounters with her foes for her deliverance. To him who dares much in this warfare God seems to give a wonderful vision of victory.

"One day about 4 years ago he was talking of an experience he had on a day of prayer that was being observed for India. He was speaking intimately to intimate friends. He said: 'On the day of prayer God gave me a new experience. I seemed to be away above our conflict here in the Punjab and I saw God's great battle in all India, and then away out beyond in China, Japan, and Africa. I saw how we had been thinking in narrow circles of our own countries and in our own denominations, and how God was now rapidly joining force to force and line to line, and all was beginning to be one great struggle. That, to me means the great triumph of Christ. We do not dare any longer to fight without the consciousness of this great world battle in which we are engaged.

"'We must exercise the greatest care to be utterly obedient to Him who sees all the battlefield all the time. It is only He who can put each man in the place where his life can count for the most.' Above all the strife of battle he could see the great Commander whom he was following so implicitly.

"When the word came to us in India that after severe suffering in America, he had been called Home, it seemed to me that I could hear something of an echo of the shout of victory as he entered into the King's presence. Then the next word that came was that he had died with the words upon his lips: '*Bol, Yisu' Masih, Ki Jai!*' ('Shout, the victory of Jesus Christ!')

"When I heard that I thought of that awful time in the life of our Lord when His foes were closing in about Him. He knew that the time of His sacrifice was near. Just before Him lay the desertion of His disciples, and Gethsemane, and Calvary. Yet in that hour He said, 'Be of good cheer, I have overcome the world.' Then I remembered the days and nights when Mr. Hyde had struggled in India for those bound by sin, and that after hours of agony he had often risen with those about him to shout: '*Bol, Yisu' Masih, Ki jai,*' until this has become the great war cry of the Punjab Church. As he sent that shout back to us from the presence of the great Victor, let us see to it that it rings throughout the whole world: 'Shout, the victory of Jesus Christ!'"

In Jehovah's Name, Amen!

Praying Hyde

PART II

A Vessel unto Honour

BY J. PENGWERN JONES

PART II

A Vessel unto Honour

In the Very Presence of God

BY one of the last mails we had a letter from a dear sister who was a missionary in India for years, and who still longs to be back if only the state of her health and home ties would allow her to come.

She says also that she is deeply touched by the account of Mr. Hyde's wonderful prayer-life, and then she gives a few words of her own reminiscences of him. "I remember," she said, "during one of the Jubblepore Conventions, at the noon-tide prayer meeting, I was kneeling near to him, and can never forget how I was thrilled with a feeling I cannot describe as he pleaded in prayer, *"Jesus, Jesus, Jesus!"* It seemed as if a baptism of love and power came over me, and my soul was humbled in the dust before the Lord. I had the privilege of meeting Mr. Hyde again in England when on his way home to America. How his influence still lives!"

Mr. M'Cheyne Paterson describes Mr. Hyde as "a great fisher for souls," and that is very true, for he not only prayed for men, but was a real angler. He would be just for a minute in a room with perhaps a perfect stranger, but it would be quite a sufficient time to open the Bible and show some wonderful passage from the Word, and quietly he would lead the person to the Saviour. We heard of a worldly lady once who thought she would have a little fun at Mr. Hyde's expense, so she asked, "Don't you think, Mr. Hyde, that a lady who dances can go to Heaven?" He looked at her with a smile, and quietly said, "I do not see how a lady can go to Heaven unless she dances," and then he dwelt on the joy of sin forgiven—the overwhelming joy, especially for one who had been living for the world and for self, and he gently appealed to her, as to whether she had experienced this joy, and went quoting the Word of God and begging of her not to be satisfied until this wonderful experience would compel her to "dance for joy." We feel sure that she never tried to get any more fun at his expense. Truly Hyde was a fisher for souls.

Dr. Chapman, the great evangelist, said after being round the world on an evangelistic tour, that it was during a season of prayer with Mr. Hyde that he realised what *real* prayer was. I believe that hundreds in India can say the same. I owe to him more than I owe to any man, for showing me what a prayer-life is, and what a real *consecrated* life is.

I shall ever praise God for bringing me into contact with him; even now I have not been able to take in all that was lived before me by him. Jesus Christ became a new ideal to me, and I had a glimpse of His prayer-life, and I had a longing, which has remained to this day, to be a real praying man.

But let me give a few reminiscences which have been indelibly impressed on my mind. The first time I met him was at Ludhiana in the Punjab, where he lived at the time. I had been invited to speak a few words on the Revival in the Khassia Hills to the Conference of the United States Presbyterian Mission, who had their annual session at the time there. I had travelled by night from Allahabad to Ludhiana, and reached there early in the morning. I was taken to have a cup of tea with the delegates and others, and I was introduced across the table to Mr. Hyde, all that he said to me was, "I want to see you; I shall wait for you at the door." There he was waiting, and his first word was, "Come with me to the prayer room, we want you there." I do not know whether it was a command or a request. I felt I *had* to go. I told him that I had travelled all night, and that I was tired, and had to speak at four o'clock, but I went with him. We found half-a-dozen persons there, and Hyde went down on his face before the Lord. I knelt down, and a strange feeling crept over me. Several prayed, and then

Hyde began, and I remember very little more. I knew that I was in the presence of God Himself, and had no desire to leave the place; in fact, I do not think that I thought of myself or of my surroundings, for I had entered a new world, and I wanted to remain there.

We had entered the room about eight o'clock in the morning; several had gone out, others had come in, but Hyde was on his face on the floor, and had led us in prayer several times. Meals had been forgotten, and my tired feeling had gone, and the Revival account and message that I was to deliver, and concerning which I had been very anxious, had gone out of my mind, until about three-thirty, when Hyde got up, and he said to me, "You are to speak at four o'clock; I shall take you to have a cup of tea." I replied that he must need a little refreshment, too, but he said, "No, I do not want any, but you must have some." We called in at my room and washed hurriedly, and then we both had a cup of tea, and it was full time for the service. He took me right to the door, then took my hand, and said, "Go in and speak, that is *your* work. I shall go back to the prayer room to pray for you, that is *my* work. When the service is over, come into the prayer room again, and we shall praise God together." What a thrill, like an electric shock, passed through me as we parted. It was easy to speak, though I was speaking through an interpreter. What I said, I do not know. Before the meeting was over, the Indian translator, overcome by his feelings and overpowered by the Spirit of God, failed to go on, and another had to take his place. I know the Lord spoke that night. He spoke to me, and spoke to many. I realised then the power of prayer; how often I had read of blessing in answer to prayer, but it was brought home to me that evening with such force that ever since I try to enlist prayer warriors to pray for me whenever I stand up to deliver His messages. It was one of the most wonderful services I ever attended, and I know that it was the praying saint behind the scenes that brought the blessing down on me.

I went back after the service to him, to praise the Lord. There was no question asked by him, whether it was a good service or not, whether men had received a blessing or not; nor did I think of telling him what blessing I had personally received and how his prayers had been answered. He seemed to know it all, and how he praised the Lord, and how easy it was for me to praise the Lord and speak to Him of the blessing He had given. I had very little talk with him at that Conference. I knew very little about him, and somehow I had no desire to ask him any questions; but a new power had come into my life which humbled me, and gave me a new idea altogether of a missionary's life, and even a Christian life, and the ideal revealed to me then has never been lost, but, with the years as they pass, there is a deeper longing to live up to the ideal.

I had a talk with several of the missionaries about him, and I found that he had been misunderstood by them, but their eyes were being opened to the fact that he was not an ordinary worker, but specially endowed with the spirit of prayer and given to India to teach men how to pray. Years afterwards I asked him whether he had realised in his early years that the missionaries were not in favour of the way he spent so much of his time in prayer, and he smiled that sweet smile which one can never forget, and said, "Oh, yes, I knew it, but they did not understand me, that was all; they never intended to be unkind." There was not one atom of bitterness as far as I could see. At the time that I came into contact with him, they spoke approvingly of his long vigils. The probability is that he was not in bed one night during that Conference, and the Lord honoured him. He was out of sight, but, in answer to his prayers, many were blessed, and I believe a new era in the history of the mission and in the history of the Punjab was commenced at that time.

How the Innermost Secret of the Prayer-life was Revealed

I SAID in the last memoir that my contact with Mr.

Hyde was one of the greatest blessings of my life; perhaps I should put it in the present tense, and say that it is *the greatest blessing*, for I feel that the blessing lasts, which shows that it was the Holy Spirit that used His beloved servant and made him a blessing not only to me, but to hundreds of others, men and women, Indians, Europeans, Americans, Christians, and non-Christians. The Spirit made him an object-lesson to us, that we might have a better idea of what was Christ's prayer-life. I hope and pray that these few imperfect reminiscences may be used of the Holy Spirit to reveal to others what is the "life of prayer," that we are called upon to enter into in these days.

Naturally, I was interested and desired to know how brother Hyde had entered into this life, what had led him to consecrate his life so absolutely to the Lord, and how he had been taught the secret of this prayer-life. It was very difficult to get him to speak about himself, but I think he understood that it was not mere curiosity that prompted the inquiry. How I wish I could describe this event as he related it. Can I give it in his own words? It was something like this:

"My father was a minister—a Presbyterian minister—and my mother a very devoted Christian with a beautiful voice which had been consecrated to the Lord. I determined when I was a youth to be a missionary, and a 'good missionary.' I wanted to shine as a great missionary. I passed through college and did very well. I graduated, and was a little proud of the 'B.A.' after my name. I was determined to master the Indian languages that I would have to learn, and I resolved not to let anything stand in the way that would hinder my becoming a great missionary. That was my ambition. This was not altogether perhaps of the flesh, but most of it was. I loved the Lord and I wanted to serve Him, and serve Him well, but 'self' was at the foundation of my ambition.

"My father had a dear friend—a brother minister—who had a deep desire to become a missionary, but his desire was not fulfilled. He was greatly interested in me, and was delighted that the son of his great friend was going out as a missionary. He loved me and I loved him and greatly admired him.

"When I got on board the steamer at New York, bound for India for my life work, I found in my cabin a letter addressed to me. It was in the handwriting of my father's friend. J opened it and read it. The words were not many, but the purport of them was this: 'I shall not cease praying for you, dear John, until you are filled with the Holy Spirit.' My pride was touched, and I felt exceedingly angry, and crushed the letter and threw it into a corner of the cabin and went up on deck in a very angry spirit.

The idea of implying that I was *not* filled with the Spirit! I was going out as a missionary, and I was determined to be a good missionary, and yet this man implied that I was not fitted and equipped for the work! I paced up and down that deck, a battle raging within. I felt very uncomfortable; I loved the writer, I knew the holy life he led, and down in my heart there was a conviction that he was right and that I was not fit to be a missionary. I went back after some time to my cabin and down on my knees to hunt for the crushed letter. Finding it, I smoothed it out, and read it again and again. I still felt annoyed, but the conviction was gaining on me that my father's friend was right and I was wrong.

"This went on for two or three days until I felt perfectly miserable. This was the goodness of the Lord answering the prayers of my father's friend, who must have claimed a victory for me. At last, in a kind of despair, I asked the Lord to fill me with the Holy Spirit, and the moment I did this, the whole atmosphere seemed to clear up. I began to see myself, and what a selfish ambition I had. It was a struggle almost to the end of the voyage, but I was determined long before the port was reached, that whatever would be the cost, I would be really filled with the Spirit. The second climax came when I was led to tell the Lord that I was willing even to fail in my language examinations in India, and be a missionary working quietly out of sight, that I would do anything and be anything, but the Holy Spirit I would have at any cost.

"On one of the first few days spent in India, while I was staying with another missionary, a brother of some experience, I went out with him to an open-air service. The missionary spoke, and I was told that he was speaking about Jesus Christ as the real Saviour from sin. When he had finished his address, a respectable-looking man, speaking good English, asked the missionary whether he himself had been thus saved. The question went home to my heart; for if the question had been asked me, I would have had to confess that Christ had not fully saved *me*, because I knew that there was a sin in my life which had not been taken away. I realised what a dishonour it would be on the Name of Christ to have to confess that I was preaching a Christ that had not delivered me from sin, though I would be proclaiming to others that He was a perfect Saviour.

"I went back to my room and shut myself in, and told the Lord that it must be one of two things: either He must give me victory over all my sins, and especially over the sin that so easily beset me, or I must return to America, and seek there for some other work. I said that I could not stand up to preach the Gospel until I could testify of its power in my own life. I was there for some time, facing the question, realising how reasonable it was, until the Lord assured me that He was able and willing to deliver me from all sin, that He had planned work for me in India. He did deliver me, and I have not had a doubt of this since. I can now stand up without hesitation to testify that He has given me victory, and I love to witness to this and to tell all of the wonderful faithfulness of Christ my Lord, my Saviour."

As far as I can remember, it was in some such words that Hyde gave me his experience. Can I ever forget his face as he told me these things, that inexpressibly sad look when he spoke of his sin, and that wonderful smile of his when he referred to the faithfulness of Christ?

In the School of Prayer—Another Lesson Learnt and Mastered

AT the Sialkot Conventions there are two prayer rooms, one for men and one for women, and prayer is constantly going on there, day and night, without intermission. Men and women separately meet there, and two or three experienced Christians are always present to help those who need help. At times persons lead in prayer just as in ordinary prayer meetings; at other times silent prayer goes on, or little groups form, and have prayer for some object that presses upon their heart. Missionaries and others bring anxious souls into the prayer room, and they are prayed for and dealt with by men who know how to lead souls into the light. The power that is felt at the Sialkot Convention is the result of the prayer room. I remember one year a missionary full of work, attending the Convention for the first time, and it was very evident that he did not feel at home at the services. He came to me about the third day and said that the Convention was on wrong lines altogether, that the leaders and speakers should be on the platform "to show themselves and encourage others," instead of hiding themselves in the prayer room all day. I told him that I did not agree with him, and asked whether he had been into the prayer room, and he said that he had turned in several times. Two days afterwards he came to me with a beaming face, and said, "Do you know, I have found out the secret of this Convention—*it is that prayer room.* I never saw anything like it!" I told him that I quite agreed with him, and we had a chat over the blessings that he had received and the new visions of Christ that he had had.

This prayer room, if I am not mistaken, was the work of the Holy Spirit through Hyde; it was he that spent the first nights on the watch-tower, but joined almost from the very first by his beloved friend and brother, M'Cheyne Paterson. I asked Hyde once how the Lord had taught him this lesson, and he said that some time before he was to speak at a Bible school one morning, and he had had no time or insufficient time for the preparation of the Bible reading, so he remained up all night to prepare the message. The next day he thought that, as he had spent a night in getting the message ready, there was need of getting *himself* ready also, and would not a night of prayer and praise be a good preparation for a real blessing the following day? It was the Holy Spirit's suggestion undoubtedly, for that night he remained in prayer the whole night, and enjoyed it so much that he repeated it the following night. Others joined him, some for a part of the time and some for the whole night. He was always careful in his preparation for his Bible readings, sermons, or Convention Addresses, but he often said that *the preparation of the Messenger* was quite as important as the preparation of the Message. What if we also realised this?

At the Sialkot Convention referred to, the Europeans were accommodated in the dormitory of the Mission Boarding School, a long narrow building, and our beds were placed so near each other that we had very little room to move about; the room was crowded between the services. My bed had been placed between Mr. Hyde and Dr. Griswald's beds, but I noticed that Hyde's bed had not been occupied at all. Hyde spent his time in the prayer room;

but one morning he rushed in and went down on his knees by his bed-side. This was in the early morning soon after dawn. I went to have *chota-hazri* (early breakfast), and came back and found him still praying. Then I went out to the prayer meeting and morning service, and came back at 11 o'clock, and found him still praying. I went in to breakfast and returned about 12.30, and lay down on my cot to rest and to watch him. I went to the afternoon service, then to tea, then to the 5 o'clock service, coming into the dormitory each time before going to a fresh service. At 6 o'clock he was still on his knees, and had been all day. As I had an hour to wait until dinner, I determined to watch him and, if he rose from his knees, I would ask him how it was possible for him to remain quiet the whole day and to pray while there was so much noise around, for people were coming in and going out the whole time, and there was a great deal of talking going on.

In half an hour or so he looked up and smiled. I sat on his bed and asked him what was the secret of all this. I also asked him to allow me to fetch him a cup of tea, but he refused tea and asked for a glass of water only. Then he said, "Let me tell you, what a vision I had—a new vision of Christ!" His face as he spoke seemed to be illuminated; he had come truly from the secret of His Presence, and I shall never forget his words, they gave me a new vision of Christ, and as he spoke to me I could not keep the tears back; at times I felt that it could not be true—that Jesus had never suffered so much for me, but as Hyde lifted Him up before me, I had to believe, and my heart went out to Christ in love and gratitude such as I had never felt before, and also in shame and sorrow that sin—my sin—had brought Jesus so low, into such suffering, and that vision of my dear Saviour is still before me. How I wish I could repeat it as Hyde brought me step by step to see Christ that evening.

A New Vision of the Master

He showed first of all what a condescension it was for (1) *Christ to become a man.* I saw something quite new in Christ "emptying Himself," leaving His glory and entering our world, our sinful world; what it must have cost Him to live in the atmosphere of sin; it was no wonder that He often escaped from the haunts of men, from the depressing, suffocating odour of sin to the mountains, to have a breath of the fresh air of Heaven. How Hyde described the environments of sin and the Holy Person living in the midst of it! I felt that even the Incarnation was an Infinite Sacrifice, even if the death on Calvary had never taken place.

Then he stopped and said, "And He took this place —became man—for *me.*" I saw the vicarious sufferings of Christ then, in a new light. After a little time he began again and said (2) *Christ became a slave for me.* He washed His disciples' feet—this was the work of a slave. He stooped and became a slave for me. Then he described the life of a slave, and how Christ in every sense of the word had voluntarily become a slave—*not like one*—but actually He became a bond-servant, a slave, He who was King of kings, who had the worship and adoration of the hosts of Heaven, a real slave on earth! "And all," said Hyde, "*for me, for me.*"

For some time he wept; we both wept, I wept at the thought of the sufferings of Christ for me, and how unfaithful I had been to Him; but Hyde was thinking of what he was going to say next, and what he said gave me such a shock that I hardly know how to repeat the words lest they should be misunderstood. Hyde continued speaking and weeping. "I saw more. I saw that my Jesus became a dog, a Pariah dog, *for me.*" Is it blasphemy to use these words? (3) *Jesus became a dog for me.* Hyde said that he was thinking of the Syrophenecian woman, and how Jesus applied the contemptible word "dog" to her and the Gentiles, and then, he said, the Holy Spirit led my thoughts to the truth that Jesus had died for the Gentiles, *for these dogs*—then it must be that Jesus had taken *the dog's place.* "At first," he said, "this was too awful to think of, but when I thought of His life, I had to come to the conclusion that the life of Christ had more of the characteristics of a dog's life, than anything else, and that is what I have been doing," he said; "worshipping Him and praising Him for this." He explained that it must have been the intention of Christ to teach this truth by this miracle; Christ would never have used the epithet "dog" of a human being without a great purpose in view, and it was this: He wanted men to realise that He had gone down, even below men, for the purpose of lifting them up.

Then Hyde showed the similarity between Christ's life and the pariah dog of the East.

Christ had *nowhere to lay His head.* That is how the dogs of the East live; they have no place which they can call "home," and Christ was homeless, and "to think of Christ suffering all for me," said Hyde.

The dogs of the East have constant kicks and blows from men, and that is how men treated our beloved Saviour, driven away from men, receiving oftentimes great unkindness at the hands of men, cruel words, scoffs, blows, and at last cruelly killed. Shall I ever forget the tenderness of Hyde as he spoke of the sufferings of Christ.

I remember nothing of the dinner that night, my impression is that we both sat on that bed for hours, speaking of Christ. I shall never forget it, and never forget the vision I had of the love of Christ, going lower and lower, suffering more and more, and *all for me.*

If we could only spend time alone with Christ, what visions we would get, how we also could speak of Him to others until they had visions of Him. The distractions of our worldly affairs, the attractions of the world, would cease to influence us as they do now. We need our quiet times with Him, and to take time, and make time, to be with Him, to see Him face to face.

The Burden of Prayer and its Sure Result

The most wonderful week of my life was the one spent in Murree with Mr. Hyde and several others of like spirit.

Murree is a hill station on the way to Cashmere. In the year 1907, several missionaries arranged to spend three or four weeks of the hot weather in this place, and the Spirit moved them to arrange for a week or ten days of waiting on the Lord while there. Others heard of this and joined them, and I had the great privilege of being with them. When I say that several of the leaders (or a better word would be the *intercessors*), from the Sialkot Convention were there, one can understand the privilege. I had the joy of sharing a tiny room with Hyde, and that room was a little Heaven to me, and the memories of it will never be effaced. We were entertained by Mr.

and Mrs. M'Cheyne Paterson, and all the other guests in the same house were of kindred spirit, so that the fellowship was almost perfect. Mr. Hyde was very full of humour which was under perfect control. The sad burdened features relaxed when he was in the company of those that shared his prayer life, and his face was lit up with joy—a Heavenly joy. The conversation at the table was most uplifting, and Hyde and others led us "into green pastures," and some of us who were only beginning to understand this life feasted on the thoughts that passed through the lips of those dear saints who lived in the secret of His presence. But Hyde's place was often vacant; we knew where he was; no one enjoyed the company of men and women more than he did, but Jesus came first—*he was afraid lest the fellowship of the saints should come between him and his Saviour.*

He was always on his knees clothed in a heavy overcoat when I went to bed, and on his knees long before I was up in the morning, though I was up with the dawn. He would also light the lamp several times in the night, and feast on some passage of the Word, and then have a little talk with the Master. He sometimes remained on his knees the whole day. At other times he would come with us to the services, and spend the time in prayer in the vestry adjoining the church. The services were full of power, every word seemed to reach the hearts of men. It was not the power of the messages, but the power of prayer that did it all. How easy it was to speak; there was an atmosphere of prayer. I would be in the vestry with him and a few others until the service commenced, and back to the vestry for prayer as soon as the service was over.

One day the burden of prayer for the Europeans of the station had fallen on Hyde; for two or three days he never went to bed nor did he go down to meals, and the food sent up to his room was generally carried down again untouched. How often he came and knelt by my bed that I might try to help him to bear the burden. On the Saturday night he was in great agony. M'Cheyne Paterson and myself remained with him. Oh, how he prayed and pleaded for the Europeans of the station. It was a vision to me of real agonising intercession; he seemed to say like Jacob of old, "I will not let Thee go," and yet in the determination there was such deep humility, such loving pleading. At two o'clock in the morning there was a knock at the door, and M'Cheyne Paterson quietly whispered to me, "I am sure that is my wife reminding me that we ought to go to bed;" but it was not so. It was a letter from a lady staying at the largest hotel in the place, asking us to have a service for Europeans in the drawing-room of the hotel. Hyde heard us reading the letter, and he jumped up from his knees and said, "That is the answer to my prayers. I *know* now that the Lord has heard me."

The servant who was entrusted with the message had gone miles in another direction, and had to come back, and found it very difficult at night to get any one to direct him to us, hence his appearance at two o'clock in the morning. He had been told that the message was urgent and a reply absolutely necessary. Hyde's face was just full of peace and joy, and he almost commanded us to accept the invitation and arrange for the service, which we did. It was not a large gathering at the hotel, and the service was not a success from a human standpoint, and yet I felt perfectly confident that the Lord was carrying out His plans and purposes, and that He was answering the prayers of His dear servant. Hyde, of course, remained in his room to pray, or rather to praise, for he was full of joy, and was not at all disappointed when we told him that not many of the hotel visitors had attended the service. He said that it was all in the Lord's hand, and He knew how to carry on His work. One at least that was at the service came to the evening service which was held by us in the Scotch church, and Mr. Hyde was present that night with such Heavenly joy in his features that it was contagious.

What a privilege it was to be with him for that

week! What lessons I learnt! His Bible was always in his hand, even when we had our morning cup of tea he regaled me with manna from the Word. When he knelt to pray, the dear old Book was always open before him, and his hands rested on it. Face to face with the Lord and resting on the promises. He had always some dainty morsel or other to give me from the Word; he always led me right to His presence when we prayed together. How is it that we have so few who live thus at all times "in the secret of His presence?" Why do we not yield ourselves to the Lord and let our life be one of prayer and communion with Him? Then we could lead others to a higher life.

From Murree we all went together to the Sialkot Convention, and probably that was one of the most wonderful Conventions ever held. Mr. Hyde took some of the morning Bible readings, which proved so helpful to those present.

Intercession—A Continuous Ministry

There is no doubt that the Sialkot Convention at one time, whatever it may be now, was one of the most wonderful gatherings of the Lord's children that ever took place, and Hyde had a great deal to do with the form it took. He was not conscious of this, but the atmosphere he brought with him seemed to affect the whole place. One felt a change coming over one as one entered the compound of the Convention. It was a spirit of prayer, and when we entered into the "prayer room" we understood the cause of the change of atmosphere.

Perhaps I should explain what this "prayer room" really is. Mr. Hyde and a few others realised the necessity of preparation for the Convention, and he felt that his work was to wait on God and plead for those who would attend. There are men in the Punjab who are specially endowed of the Spirit to organise such gatherings.

Dr. Gordon, on whom in the old days the great burden of organising all the departments of work fell, was so guided and helped by the Spirit that everything went like clockwork. To cater for 2000 people is not an easy task, but the arrangements were so perfect that Dr. Gordon and all his willing assistants, including the missionary ladies that superintended the commissariat, were able to attend the services. I remember Dr. Gordon telling me that he had really nothing to do except to enjoy the Convention. He spent much time in the prayer room, and one day he took me into his little tent, and showed me his account books, beautifully written, and everything noted down. The previous year's account had balanced to a *pice*, and all the work was carried on without any bustle or worry.

Why do I mention these things in writing about

Praying Hyde? Because prayer had so much to do with it. Hyde and his companions were in a room on the ground praying when Dr. Gordon and his companions were putting up the scores of tents, arranging the cooking apparatus, the supply of water, and the one hundred and one little details necessary. Hyde felt and caused others to feel that it was necessary to prepare the messages and the tents and the food and the sleeping accommodation and, when others reached the ground to arrange the external necessities, he was on the ground to enter the prayer room, and for two or three days and nights, Hyde and a few others were on their faces praying, pleading, praising, and claiming a blessing.

Has the marquee been erected? Hyde and his party enter in at once to dedicate it to the Lord, and to make the spot a real Bethel where God would meet with His people. Is the dining-tent in position? The praying party must be there at once, so that the Spirit of God can use the meal-times to bring blessing to His people. Sometimes the conversation in the dining-tent destroys the effect of the messages given in the preaching-tent; but in Sialkot we never heard any gossip during meal-times. Men and women formed parties, Indians and Europeans together, sitting at tables or in small groups on the floor eating their meal, and feasting on the fellowship in the Lord. Was there any one in spiritual difficulties? Some brother or sister would say, "Let us go together to have a little food and talk over this great matter," and there, while eating, they realised that Jesus was with them; the meal was sanctified by His presence, and everything appeared in a new light. Some one has found the Saviour, and the Lord must be praised and a hymn or a Bhajan is started, and in an instant the whole place is full of praise. The ladies giving out the food, the Christian waiters, as well as those who are eating, all unite in praising God. The Punjabis can sing, and the missionaries can sing, too. It was in the dining-tent I heard the "Glory Song" sung in a way that I shall never forget, and I longed to go to "Glory" there and then to begin this glory life. The food was left and got cold before we could eat it, but our hearts had been warmed up with the fire of His love burning within. Had Hyde's prayer anything to do with this? I do not know, but I do know that this is what he and his companions prayed for.

The first day of the Convention, and often on the previous night, the two prayer rooms were open, one for men and one for women, and prayer and praise went on continually until two or three days after the Convention. It is immediately after the seed is sown that the birds come and devour the seed, "*then* cometh the Devil, and taketh away the Word out of their hearts" (Luke 8. 12). M'Cheyne Paterson always says the the time for very earnest definite prayer is *immediately after* the service or a Convention is over, and Hyde believed in this, and so when others remained on the ground after the Convention was over to pull down the tents, etc., the prayer room parties remained to plead that the results of the Convention might be permanent.

If we had more prayer in the very place of our conferences and assemblies before they commence, during the sessions, and when they are over, how different the atmosphere would be! If we only realised that there is *as much need for heart-preparation as there is for comfort-preparation*; if we could feel that this is the absolute necessity, and for some to take this burden upon them as Hyde did, what a blessing we would have! Can we not take this lesson to heart?

Within the Veil

Let us look at Hyde in the prayer room, say, in the Sialkot Convention. The prayer room is in the Scottish church. Some of the seats have been moved aside, and a carpet covers this open space. Sometimes there are hundreds of people there, at other times only two or three. Right on his face on the ground is "Praying Hyde"—this was his favourite attitude for prayer. Listen! He is praying—he utters a petition, and then waits; in a little time he repeats it, and then waits, and this many times, until we all feel that the petition has penetrated into every fibre of our nature, and we feel assured that God has heard and without a doubt He will answer. How well I remember him praying that we might "open our mouth wide that He might fill it" (Psa. 81. 10). I think he repeated the word "wide" scores of times, with long pauses between, "Wide, Lord," "Wide," "Open wide," "Wide." How effectual it was to hear him address God, "Oh, Father! Father!" Even before he asked anything I always felt that the Father knew what he was going to ask for.

When he finished his prayer, perhaps half-a-dozen are sobbing. Hyde goes to one of them, and others who are present go to the others. Hyde's arm is around the neck of the one that he is going to deal with; he speaks but little, but his well-worn Bible is used, and before long he stands up with a smile, and the man with him, and he begins to sing: "'Tis done, the great transaction's done," and he is so full of joy that his whole body begins to move, he claps his hands, and then his feet begin to move, and look! he begins to dance for joy, and others join him until the whole place rings with God's praises.

Sometimes he wants to be alone, and I heard of him climbing into the belfry; there, in the dark, high above the others, he pours out his soul to God. Men hear the echo of his voice, and realise that he must not be disturbed, for he is wrestling with God.

What about his meals, and his bed? The Convention lasted for ten days in those early days, and his "boy," a lad about sixteen that he had taken to his home and his heart, had brought Hyde's bedding and had carefully made his bed, but it was never used during the Convention. I saw him more than once, when the prayer room was full, go aside into one of the corners and throw himself on the floor to sleep, but if the room began to get empty and prayer to flag, he somehow seemed to know it and was up immediately and took his place with the other intercessors. Did he go to his meals? I think it was only once or twice that I saw him with us at table. Sometimes his "boy," or Gulla, the sweeper, or one of his friends would take a plate of curry and rice or something else to him to the prayer room, and if convenient he would go to a corner and eat it. How his "boy" used to cry because he would not eat properly and would not go to bed to sleep.

Hyde was not the only one that did this; there were other missionaries who did the same, and Indian workers also, but it was Hyde's spirit and example that first of all led them into this "prayer life." How often Hyde told me that he was afraid of following the example of men, and *he dreaded lest any one should try to follow his example*, or M'Cheyne Paterson's example, and so I wish to close this chapter of reminiscences by begging of our readers to follow

Hyde in his prayer-life and prayer-spirit, but not necessarily in the "form" that he manifested it.

There are thousands of God's children who cannot spend weeks in prayer and fasting as he did; they are physically unfit for it; but every one can have this prayer-life, making prayer their very breath. We need to be in the line of God's will in this as in every other duty. Hyde realised that in his case God demanded it of him. We all feel our need of more prayer, and to be more persistent in prayer and intercession, whether we spend a night or a month on our knees. Realising my own need, may I ask my fellow-workers, Indians and Europeans, especially at this time, shall we not give more of our time to prayer? *Can we not have an occasional day of prayer and fasting?* Let us go to the Lord and settle it with Him. Let us be willing to sacrifice our own comforts in order to have more time for prayer.

A Living Message from the Empowered Messenger

I wrote about Hyde at the Conventions, and promised to give one or two other incidents which I observed at the Conventions. He felt that his place was in the prayer room, but he had to enter the platform at times, and his messages were delivered with tremendous power, as we would naturally expect when he came straight from the prayer room to deliver his message. I shall never forget the effect of one of his Bible readings on the congregation, and on the whole Convention.

He spoke in Urdu, and those who know Urdu say that he spoke the language well, if anything a little highflown, using the book-language more than the colloquial. I could not follow him, for my knowledge of Urdu is very meagre, so I had an opportunity of watching him and the congregation. I realised very soon that he was delivering a solemn message, for there was a solemnity in the congregation that was almost oppressive. He spoke quietly, but all could hear him, and I felt that his *life* was in the word.

He once told me that one had to give *himself* if he wanted to serve God and help men, that it was not enough to give our time and our talents, that our "life" must be given. This was true, he said, both in praying and in preaching. Alas! how few of us give of our life; when we think that our life is touched, we feel it is time to draw back. How often we have heard it said, "You will kill yourself if you work as you do; take it easy." But Hyde used to say, "Give your life for God and men." Let that vital energy, that living power within, be poured out for men. Who was right? Hyde or the modern man? Hyde gave himself as he preached—he poured out his life as he prayed . . . that morning in Sialkot he did this, and men realised the power. I heard that immediately after the service, the committee was called together to consider God's challenge to them, and for prayer that the message might influence men. At breakfast, men were in groups, asking what should be done, and I know that many went away alone to have their lives readjusted by the Holy Spirit.

At one of the Conventions he spoke to the Europeans. Most of them were missionaries. He spoke on "The Cross." I think that the Spirit used him to give us all an entirely new vision of the Cross. That was one of the most inspiring messages I ever heard. He began the address by saying that from whatever side or direction we look at Christ on the Cross, we see wounds, we see signs of suffering—from above we see the marks of the crown of thorns, from behind the Cross we see the furrows caused by the scourging, etc., and he dwelt on the Cross with such illumination that we forgot Hyde and every one else, the "dying, yet living Christ" was before us. Then step by step we were led to see in the crucified Christ a sufficiency for every need of ours, and as he dwelt on the fitness of Christ for *every* emergency, I felt that I had sufficient for time and for eternity.

But the climax of all to me was the way he emphasised the truth that Christ on the Cross cried out triumphantly, "IT IS FINISHED," when all around thought that His life had ended. It seemed to His disciples that He had failed to carry out His purposes;

it appeared to His enemies that at last their dangerous Enemy had been overcome. To all appearances the struggle was over and His life had come to a tragic end. Then the triumphant cry of victory was sounded out, "IT IS FINISHED." A cry of triumph in the darkest hour.

Then Hyde showed us that if united to Christ we can also shout triumphantly, even when everything points to despair. Though our work may appear to have failed, and the enemy to have gained the ascendancy, and we are blamed by all our friends and pitied by all our fellow-workers, *even then* we can take our stand with Christ on the Cross and shout out, "Victory, victory, victory!" From that day I have never been in despair about our work. Whenever I feel despondent, I think I hear Hyde's voice shouting "Victory!" and that immediately takes my thought to Calvary, and I hear my Saviour in His dying hour, crying out with joy, "IT IS FINISHED." As Hyde said, *"This is real victory,"* to shout triumphantly though all around is darkness.

I remember that the Hon. M. Waldegrave (the late Lord Radstock's son), was in the service, and in leaving at the close, he said to me, "I generally go to my tent after every service and write the message that I have heard to my wife, but Mr. Hyde's message just delivered seems so sacred and appealing that I dare not try to write it."

I had a long talk with Hyde afterwards about the Cross and the message, and he told me that for a whole year he had been fascinated by the Cross. "I cannot speak on any other subject now," he said. I heard him speak on the Cross at another Convention some weeks afterwards, and that was accompanied by the Holy Spirit's power in a similar way.

How the Spirit of Dissension was Quenched at Sialkot

At the first Convention that I attended at Sialkot, the Evil One made a desperate attempt to destroy the whole work. At the previous Convention some terrible confessions had been made both by missionaries and Indian workers, and at the Convention that I attended, sins were revealed that shocked all persons present. Some few that attended were exceedingly annoyed, and wanted the committee to consider the question and decide either that there should be no public confession, or else that men and women should be separated, and men should confess at the men's meetings, and women at the women's meetings. These people wanted the committee to meet them to discuss the whole matter. The reply of the committee was, "Let us meet together to pray over the matter." These men would not, and said that it was useless to pray until the question had been decided. As I was an outsider, I heard the arguments on both sides. I did not like to hear open confession of the sins of immorality, but I deplored the spirit manifested by some of the people who were against confessions. One young fellow, thumping the table, said, "I'll smash the whole Convention."

I had a quiet talk on the subject with Hyde. He was one of the committee, and manifested such a tender, loving spirit and was so sane through it all, that I was greatly impressed. He said that the committee had never called for confessions, *that it was the Spirit of God that had moved men to confess.* He said that he felt that legislation on the question, and setting apart special meetings for confessions, would be like taking the matter out of the Holy Spirit's hand, and it would in one way give sanction to open confession. I well remember how earnestly he said that the sin of immorality was more prevalent among the Christians than any one dreamt, and that the Holy Spirit saw that *extreme measures were needed to get men to realise the sin.* "Some men, I fear," said Hyde, "are guilty, and are afraid that the Holy Spirit will compel them to confess." How tenderly he spoke of these men, how confident he was that the Lord at the right moment would reveal clearly His will in the matter; it was one of the darkest hours of the Sialkot Convention, and yet Hyde's face was full of joy, for he knew that victory was assured.

Victory came; those who opposed confession went together to the prayer room, hoping to discuss the question. Hyde was praying, several others of the committee were praying, and they gave such a hearty welcome to those men to pray with them that they did so, and after some time, M'Cheyne Paterson, one of the members of the committee, spoke, and spoke with such power that the discussion dropped. He showed that no member of the committee had ever urged public confession. All that the committee desired was implicit obedience to the Holy Spirit. These men said that they, too, desired that all men should obey the Spirit, and then some one began to praise God, and all joined in singing, and the prayer room became once more a praise room.

I realised then in a new way how much better it would be to settle our differences by meeting together to pray, by allowing the Holy Spirit to have His way with us. Since then I have put this matter more than once to the test. When at committee meetings or conferences disputes arose and feelings ran high, when men began to get excited and fight for their own opinions, the best way to meet all this was to keep quiet in a corner, praying that the Holy Spirit might come and reveal His will and direct men's thoughts in the right path, how wonderfully He has led us out of the mazes and brought peace and happiness to men's minds.

This was Hyde's way of meeting difficulties, and this was the way of the Master. Shall this be our way? Whatever may be the trouble, let us put ourselves in the right attitude towards God, and then wait for the Holy Spirit to work in us to do what is right.

A Resting-Time in Wales

I left for Wales in December, 1910. I saw Mr. Hyde the previous October, and knew that he intended taking his furlough early in 1911. I asked him to take a run across to see me when passing through England, and he replied, as he generally did, that he would call if the Lord would open the way. I gave him my address, but he lost it. The day before his steamer was due to arrive in Liverpool he asked a C.M.S. missionary who was on board whether he had any idea what part of Wales I came from. I had only a casual acquaintance with this missionary, and had never seen his wife, but he immediately told Hyde that his wife had my address, and he went down to her cabin and brought it up. To this day I have no idea where she obtained my address.

The steamer arrived in Liverpool on Good Friday, and he crossed over to Birkenhead to get a train for my home (Llangollen). When he reached the station he was told that only one train ran on Good Friday, and that had gone. Some one overheard the question and answer, and told him that there was a cheap excursion train going direct to the place, and told him to book an excursion ticket, which he did, but, when he reached the train, he was told that he could take no luggage with him, and he had all his belongings in a big American trunk. He waited a moment, and prayed, I am sure, when the guard came to him, and said, "Go and secure your seat, and leave your trunk with me. I shall bring it in my van," and he did so. All these incidents I have mentioned were clear indications to him *that he was in the line of God's will.* He lived so near the Lord that he was sensitive to the slightest promptings of His will, and he seemed to know at once when the Lord was not with him. How everything fitted together because all was under the direct control of God for the good of His servant!

But this was not all. It had been arranged by the Mission that I should be on deputation work for some time in Carnarvonshire just those days, but at the last moment the tour was cancelled, because the people were too busy in arranging for the installation of the Prince of Wales as Prince in Carnarvon, for arrangements to be made for missionary meetings, and so I had a fortnight's rest in my old home, and I wondered what was behind all this. I was glad of the quiet time, but I felt there was some other reason.

On Good Friday morning I went round the little town just as I used to go when I was a boy, and told my wife that I would be back in less than an hour, but when I arrived back, my wife rushed to the door, and said, "Guess who has come? Of all your numerous friends, which one would you like to see and have his company on Good Friday?" I could not mention any one, but I felt that there was some joy in store for me, and I saw that my wife was greatly excited, for she had longed for years to meet Hyde. Then she said, "Go to the bedroom and see who is there having a wash." I rushed upstairs, and there was Hyde, with his face beaming with joy, and that was the beginning of a month or two of a little Heaven on earth for me.

It was not difficult for me to persuade him to make his home with me for some weeks. A dearly beloved doctor and his wife who lived near begged that they should entertain him, and as I knew that he would be far more comfortable there than in the little house where we stayed, and I knew that he needed the care of a doctor, we gladly allowed them to have him there to sleep, and he came for most of his meals to us. What a time that was! He and my wife seemed to understand each other from the very first hour, and no brother and sister in the Lord ever loved each other, and understood each other, better than they did. What time we spent around that little table, where we had our meals! The fellowship was so sweet, the blessing asked for before the meal commenced often turned into a lengthy prayer, and the food became cold, but our hearts were warmed up, and every morsel we ate seemed to be tasty and to have an additional relish. What a privilege it is to have one of the children of God who lives in His very presence with us at the table. It became the Lord's banqueting house, and we freely drank of His Spirit. What would I not give to have one of those days back again! Will my readers forgive me for dwelling so long on this? I had such a blessing I can never forget it.

We went round to visit some of the old saints, and, among others, we called on a dear aged child of God who was very deaf. Mr. Hyde himself was deaf. This dear old lady shouted to him, that she missed the services very much, "for I cannot hear anything when I go," she said, and to her surprise he said, "You ought to praise God for that." She thought that he had misunderstood her, and she said again, "I *cannot* hear, I tell you," and he answered, "That is why I tell you that you should praise the Lord." Then he explained to her what he meant. He said that it was rarely that he could hear anything when he went to the services, but that it was a fine opportunity to pray, everything was so quiet and the whole environment seemed to help him to pray and worship. He said that he looked at the preacher and prayed for him, then at the different people, and prayed for them as he looked at them, until he began to praise God for being deaf, as it gave him such a glorious opportunity for prayer and adoration. The dear old lady laughed heartily and entered into the spirit of his remarks, and said quite cheerfully, "I think I shall try that way, too." And some two or three years afterwards she wrote to me and said that she praised God for what Hyde had said, and that it had made a wonderful difference in her life. She has gone Home, and no doubt they have been drawn together on the other side and praise God together for all the way that He led them.

What walks we had together on the mountain side, and we would sit down together on one of the rustic seats provided for visitors, and have a time of prayer together, or throw ourselves down under some of those shady trees, and have fellowship with the Master. How one longs for Him!

It was during some of these walks that he gave me some of his early history. He spoke a great deal about his mother, what an earnest Christian she was, and what careful training she had given him. He often spoke of her singing; and over and over again he said that she was the best singer he had ever heard, and such a holy woman. I felt at the time that he just longed to go home to her.

When he was staying with me, he often spoke of Keswick, and his one desire then was to remain in England over Keswick Week. He wanted to attend the Convention, and to have M'Cheyne Paterson with him there, and he was giving me the privilege of being with them so as to make a trio, and we were to have a prayer room in *Keswick* during the Convention, and to continue in prayer day and night. However, both he and M'Cheyne Paterson were ill during the Convention, and failed to attend. The Lord allowed me to go there, but we did not have the prayer room, though I did suggest it. I often think what would have been the result if they had come there. Mr. Walker of Tinnevelly was present, and would certainly have joined us. To this day the "prayer room" has not had its place at Keswick, but there has been so much prayer for this, that it may yet come, and then Keswick will be as near perfection as we can imagine any holy gathering this side of Paradise.

Victory Over the Powers of Darkness

One of the red-letter days in my friendship with Hyde was in connection with one of the missions which Chapman and Alexander conducted in one of the towns in Western England. Mr. Hyde was staying with us in my home, and we happened to be without deputation work for some days, and we heard that a mission was to be conducted by Messrs. Chapman and Alexander, and I suggested that we should attend this mission for three days. We engaged small rooms in a quiet hotel. For the first afternoon we had two of the Lord's children with us, a man and wife who had been greatly blessed in the 1904-5 Revival, and Mr. Hyde's company was made a great blessing to them.

Mr. Hyde had never met Mr. Chapman, but, as they both belonged to the same Church, Mr. Hyde was anxious to meet him. We reached the town (Shrewsbury) about midday on a Thursday. The first service was to be held at two o'clock. After a little food we made our way towards the service, so as to secure a good seat, as we expected a great throng. It was some little disappointment to me personally to find the street comparatively empty.

When in sight of the hall we saw Mr. Chapman and party coming, and we waited for them, and Mr. Hyde immediately went and introduced himself to Mr. Chapman. Possibly Mr. Chapman had heard his name as a missionary of his own Church, but little did he guess the help that this missionary was to render him in his mission and his life. Very few people were in the hall, but a few more came by two o'clock.

There was nothing very remarkable in the service; it was good, and I enjoyed it, but we were all so disappointed at the congregation, that we all felt more or less depressed. I met one of the ministers, and expressed my disappointment, and he said that such missions were not popular in their town, and evidently he was very well satisfied. At night we had a larger congregation, but there was no enthusiasm. We thoroughly enjoyed the service, but were surprised at the lack of zeal and response at the meeting. It was very evident that Mr. Chapman and the others who were helping him were also disappointed. Hyde said very little. That night one of the leading elders of one of the Churches, an old friend of mine, joined us at supper, and he was surprised that we had come all the way to attend a mission. He had heard of it, but had not attended the meetings. We persuaded him to interest himself in the work, and he promised to attend *if he could.*

It was suggested by Mr. Chapman that the ministers and leaders should meet together the next day for a quiet talk and prayer to see whether anything could be done to rouse the people to attend the services. Mr. Hyde and myself were asked to be present, and it was at this meeting that we realised the great need of prayer. The ministers present, and they were a good number, seemed to treat the whole mission as some little side-show. Mr. Chapman's address was intense, but the remarks made by some of the ministers revealed a state of appalling indifference, so that even Dr. Chapman with a sad countenance said that if that was the spirit in which the leaders faced the mission, that he had nothing more to say, and asked the people to excuse him, and went out. That to some extent sobered the most frivolous, and the few earnest souls had their way. I noticed Hyde's head getting lower and lower, and his face wore that burdened look he always had when the burden of prayer was coming on him. He spoke but little to any one that night, and the next afternoon we had to leave, for we both had preaching engagements on the Sunday; but he came to me and asked me to engage his room for him for the following week, that he intended coming back on Monday morning.

"I cannot leave a brother minister to bear this burden alone," he said. I secured the room for him. He spoke with power at two or three services on the Sunday, and returned by train early on Monday. Knowing the weak state of his health, and fearing lest the burden should be too much for him, I wrote (unknown to Hyde) a line to Dr. Chapman, asking him, if possible, to arrange for some one to be with Hyde, so as to help him in his work of intercession. Mr. Chapman very kindly arranged for a worthy, sympathetic helper in the person of Mr. Davis, of the Pocket Testament League, and the two being kindred spirits became very friendly.

What was the result of this intercession? Let Mr. Chapman's letter tell.

"At one of our missions in England the audience

was extremely small. Results seemed impossible, but I received a letter from a missionary that an American missionary known as 'Praying Hyde,' would be in the place to pray God's blessing down upon our work. Almost instantly the tide changed—the hall was packed, and my first invitation meant fifty men for Jesus Christ. As we were leaving, I said, 'Mr. Hyde, I want you to pray for me.' He came to my room, turned the key in the door, dropped on his knees, waited five minutes without a single syllable coming from his lips. I could hear my own heart thumping and his beating. I felt the hot tears running down my face. I knew I was with God. Then with upturned face, down which tears streamed, he said, 'Oh, God!' Then for five minutes at least he was still again, and then when he knew that he was talking to God, his arm went round my shoulder, and then came up from the depth of his heart such petitions for men as I have never heard before, and I rose from my knees to know what *real* prayer was. We have gone round the world and back again, believing that prayer is mighty, and we believe it as never before."

Mr. Hyde remained in the place for a whole week, and then crawled back to us. I saw at once that he had been wrestling with the Lord and had gained the victory, but it had almost been too much for his physical strength. The following day he could scarcely speak, he was so weak! But he smiled and whispered to me as I bent over him, "The burden was very heavy, but my dear Saviour's burden for me took Him down to the grave."

From other sources we heard what a great success the mission had been, how the churches were revived and many were brought to the Light. I was specially glad to read of a stirring address given at a Presbytery a few weeks afterwards by the very elder who had joined us at supper and was scarcely interested enough to attend the mission; but he did attend, and was gloriously blessed, and his account of the mission and the blessing which accompanied it stirred the whole Presbytery. How much had Hyde's prayer to do with this?

Thinking over Hyde's share in the work, I could not help comparing his devotion and my lack of responsibility. He realised the need in a way that I did not. He was willing to sacrifice everything so that Christ's Name should be honoured in that town. How willing he was to work out of sight; he never thought of himself, he just saw the town, the condition of the churches, the indifference of the ministers, as Christ Himself saw these things, and instead of criticising and blaming the men, he took their burden and carried it to the Lord. Not one word of criticism did I hear, not one word of what he had done, but he did speak of the glory of Christ manifested, of the powerful messages delivered by Messrs. Chapman and Alexander, and especially of the power of intercession which his companion Mr. Davies had received. Oh, for that absence of self in me! For the power of prayer, and the Spirit's insight to see the need all around!

Triumphing under Testings

Two incidents which occurred when Mr. Hyde was in England gave me great pain, but they did not appear to affect him in any way; and to watch him at that time made me realise how very Christ-like he was, and brought home many lessons to me.

Hyde and myself were invited to join the Keswick speakers and promoters in a two-days' prayer meeting at the residence of the late Evan Hopkins. We were glad of the invitation, and had two days of very precious fellowship with the Lord and the dear saints assembled (about forty or more). The time was spent in prayer—it was an ideal time of intercession. I could see that the burden of prayer had come upon Hyde, for his very countenance proved it. He was in his element with so many experienced intercessors around him. But I saw that he longed that they should be led into a still deeper life of intercession. He did not say so, for criticism was not in his line at all. I do not think that I ever heard him criticising any persons, though he could vehemently denounce sin. It was by his prayers, when we were praying together, that I was led to realise this. Towards the middle of the second day, one or two spoke, and there was a kind of discussion over the question of a prayer room for Keswick, and we were asked to state our experience of this in Indian conventions. I stated very briefly my thoughts on the subject. I wanted Hyde to have as much time as possible, for I felt that he would raise the question to a much higher level than the setting apart of a prayer room, where continued prayer could be made.

He began, and spoke more slowly, if anything, than usual. I happened to be the only one that knew him, and knew by his manner that he was heavily burdened with his message. He spoke very quietly for three or four minutes, then one of the ladies present began to sing a popular hymn, and it was taken up by several others, *and the message was never delivered.* Mr. Hyde just closed his eyes and prayed. I was afraid that his feelings would have been hurt, but there was not a word of resentment or even displeasure. How many of us would have borne it as he did? The burden weighed so heavily upon him that he was prostrated, and had a violent headache and became so weak that he could not leave with the rest of us that evening, so he stayed on as the guest of Mr. Evan Hopkins, and he told me afterwards that he had such blessed fellowship with him.

Not one word did he utter about the meeting having sung him down, but spoke with love and tenderness of all. How many of us would have stood it in the same way? I am afraid I would have keenly felt it even if I had not resented it; but Hyde's constant fellowship with Christ in prayer had made him impervious even to such subtle attacks of the Evil One.

A similar incident took place at a Presbytery in North Wales. Mr. Hyde had been speaking with great power at many of the churches belonging to that Presbytery, and many were the invitations that he had to be present at the following Presbytery and deliver a message to the ministers and elders. He was not officially asked by the moderator, but the leaders in the church where the Presbytery was held had pressed him to be present. Being a Presbyterian himself, he told me that he looked forward with joy to the gathering. It was at a great sacrifice that he attended; he had to leave very early in the morning and take a long railway journey so as to be in time. He was suffering, too, at the time from a severe headache and from the malady which carried him away in less than twelve months. The Presbytery was a large one, for it was rumoured that Hyde would be present. Word was sent up to the moderator and to the secretary more than once, but the meeting closed without even welcoming a brother Presbyterian minister, who had been a missionary for years to their midst. A visitor is usually welcomed, especially if his name be known, but Mr. Hyde sat out throughout the whole meeting. Being deaf he could not hear, and the proceedings being carried on in Welsh, he would not have understood had he been able to hear. His eyes were closed, and I knew he was praying for all present. When the meeting closed and many rushed up to him to shake hands with him and to express their disappointment that he had not been asked to speak, he smiled on all and spoke quite cheerfully, and when I expressed my sorrow and my indignation to him when we were alone, he gently rebuked me and said that the Lord knew everything, and it was not our place to criticise the Lord's people.

Scores of times since then have I thought of him when the Lord's children were inclined to act unkindly towards me, or appeared to me to misunderstand my attitude wilfully, and been compelled to check myself and not to criticise them, but to praise the Lord that He knew all and to pray for the very friends that acted so.

How often Mr. Hyde excused men who had been unkind to him. "They do not understand," he said. "I know they do not want to be unkind," he once replied when he was asked to defend himself against a bitter and unjust attack. A friend even offered to write and explain, but he quietly said,

"This is my cross which He wants me to take up and carry for Him."

What if we all had this spirit—misunderstandings in mission stations, etc., would cease. How the work in many stations in India is marred and hindered by these trivial misunderstandings. The parties themselves grieve over this and wish it could be removed. How often the work of the Holy Spirit has been hindered and even stopped by petty jealousies; some one feeling that he is not having the position he ought to have, or some one has passed an unkind remark or an uncharitable criticism about some one else. Oh, these petty quarrels, jealousies, and misunderstandings among the dear children of God. How can they be done away with? I think that Hyde's way is sure to succeed. Be much in prayer: let any slight or even insult be an occasion to pray for the very persons that do these things, and praise God for the privilege of being permitted to bear these things. I think it is Madam Guyon that used to say when she was insulted or persecuted, "Thank you, Father; you saw I needed just this humbling."

But we need a *life* of prayer to be able to do this, not a spasmodic spurt, but a *habit* of prayer, to live in communion with Him. Shall we take this lesson from Hyde?

His Three Outstanding Characteristics

Thinking over Mr. Hyde's life as a whole, I find some special features in him which account for his influence over men.

1. *His ardent love for the Saviour.* I asked Hyde one day how it was that he was not married, that a wife would be able to look after his comforts. He smiled and, after a little time, he said, just as if he were betraying a secret:

"Years ago I felt that I wanted to give something to Jesus Christ who loved me so, and I gave myself to Him absolutely, and promised Him that no one should come into my life and share my affection for Him. I told the Lord that I would not marry, but be His altogether."

What a devotion! and how loyally he kept his promise. Christ was all in all to him, he was constantly talking to Him; this accounted for the atmosphere of prayer that Hyde lived in. This love was a gift, and we can have the same gift; Hyde went down lower and lower, so that the love of God could be *poured* into his life; he opened his life for God's love to flow in. Oh, that we could do this, then prayer would naturally flow into our lives also.

2. Arising out of this, all knew that *he had a passionate love for the people among whom he worked,* so that he practically sacrificed everything for them. He lived with them, he ate and slept with them.

I repeatedly heard that some took advantage of his kindness and imposed upon him. He knew this, but would say nothing to them, even though they stole his goods. He saw men wearing his clothes: he would not call them to account lest the men should be driven farther away from Christ. He so loved men's souls that worldly goods were of no account when a soul was in danger. He was often blamed for this by some of his fellow-missionaries, but it had no effect upon him. An Indian doctor in the Punjab told me soon after Mr. Hyde's Home-call that some time before, the Arya Samaj was troubled because of his influence over men and the number of men that were converted under his preaching. The members of the Samaj determined to send a man to find out all about Mr. Hyde's life, to watch for his faults, and then they would publish these abroad and so break his influence over the people.

One of their number went to Mr. Hyde and pretended that he was an inquirer, and wanted to know all about the Christian religion. Mr. Hyde received him kindly and invited him to stay with him. This was just what the man wanted, and he remained with Mr. Hyde for three or four days, and then ran away, and went to the men that had sent him and said, *"He has no fault, the man has no fault, he is a God! he is a God, and not man!"* This was the verdict of a man who lived with him day and night for three or four days—*no fault.* How many of us would have stood the test? He so loved men, and men realised it, that they could see no fault in him. This again accounted for his prayer life. Hyde must have seen much fault in the men, but to see a fault was only an excuse for prayer for those men. He always found some excuse for those who deceived and robbed him; it was so like the Master, "They know not what they do."

If we loved men more and sacrificed more for them, we would pray more for them.

3. *His genuine regard and affection for his fellow-missionaries,* and yet he dared to go against their opinions when he felt that the Lord was guiding him in that direction. We have heard some of the members of his own mission say that for years they did not understand him, but once they did they were the first to acknowledge his power. Some hard things were said to him and of him, but I do not think that any one ever heard him speak an unkind word *to* any missionary or *of* a missionary. He said more than once to me that some of the missionaries did not understand him. Many thought that he was a morose, melancholy person, but he was not, though he looked like that at times. When he was in the company of those that understood him, how bright and cheerful he was; he had what some have called "sanctified humour." He was very humorous,

but he had it under perfect control, and he seemed to keep the company that he was in in the same spirit.

His influence over missionaries the last few years of his life was wonderful. I think that it would not be wrong to say that he created a new era of prayer in the Punjab among some of the old prayer warriors that knew and felt India's needs. They prayed much for the country, and loved to be with Mr. Hyde, for he gave them a new conception of prayer; the dear Indian Christians flocked around him, and he always gave them some dainty morsel from the Word. He was as faithful in leading men to Christ; if he thought that men were looking up to him and not to the Master, he would run away and remain away in some hiding-place praying for them.

"He being dead yet speaketh" is true of him. It is now many years since he was called Home, but he is not forgotten; he is speaking to us to-day, and throwing light on the prayer life of Christ. Whenever I spent a few days in his company, I always vowed that I would pray more than I had ever done, and Christ always seemed more real to me; it seemed easy to pray, for Jesus had become more precious than ever to me. And if these reminiscences of him will lead us nearer to Christ and give us a new conception of prayer, then they will not have been written in vain.

Praying—Preaching—Persuading

We do not know of any three words that describe him better than the words, "Praying, Preaching, Persuading." This was the sum and substance of his life, and if we could bring ourselves and get others to make this to be our very life, what a blessing it would be to India and to the world.

PRAYING. Our difficulty is to keep the prayer balance of our work, to keep duties in their right relation, to put *first things first.* We have been told over and over again, and we have often told ourselves this, though we may not have said so openly, that duties are so pressing that we have no time to give to prayer as we ought to give. We all acknowledge the importance of prayer, but we excuse ourselves for not giving more time to intercession by saying that duties have been given to us and we *must* attend to them, and if we gave some hours to prayer it would mean the neglect of those duties. But if we probe down to the real cause we shall find that it is not so much the duties that press upon us as the fear of men; we wonder what would men think of us, and say about us, if we apparently fail to carry on the work entrusted to us or postpone it. It would sometimes lead others into trouble and they would blame us. But Hyde had learnt to put God first, and would allow himself to be misunderstood rather than neglect prayer. Sometimes the burden of prayer would be upon him, and during those days letters would reach him, but Hyde felt that he had to concentrate his whole life on prayer and to attend to his correspondence would be a distraction. He was not one that wilfully neglected his correspondence, but when this interfered with his prayer life it had to be kept in abeyance. Sometimes he had been announced to speak, but the burden of prayer would come, and he dare not go, so men would be disappointed, and some would be annoyed.

He was careful in keeping his engagements; labour, sleep, money, would gladly be sacrificed in order to keep his engagements, but nothing would move him when the burden of prayer came upon him. Do we put prayer first? Should we not readjust our lives so that we can give time to prayer? Is not this the great cause of our lack of power? The prophet Isaiah says that the cause of failure is our sin. "*Your iniquities have separated between you and your God, and your sins have hid His face from you, that He will not hear.*" How true this is. We cannot pray, we cannot be alone with God while we knowingly, wilfully harbour sin in our life. The sin must go if we are going to plead with God. One of the Lord's servants who is filled with the Spirit and with power told us how he entered into this experience; he realised his need and was miserable, so he determined that he would shut himself in his room and "have it out" with God, but no sooner had he dropped on his knees than God said, "Give up this habit of yours." He felt angry with himself for being so childish and sentimental, but he could not pray, and left the room, but he felt so miserable that he tried again, with the same result, and this went on for some days. At last, in a kind of despair, he told the Lord that he would give up everything, though he did not believe that the habit had anything to do with his failure, but if the Lord wanted it removed, he was willing for the Lord to do so, as he could not do it himself, and instantly the whole atmosphere changed, and he had access to the Lord, and every day he was drawn to the secret place. Many other sins during the following days were revealed to him while on his knees, but it was not difficult to part with these sins.

Perhaps our sins hinder our prayers; we may be very sure that we cannot keep on long in secret prayer while we nurse secret sins in our lives. But what we wish to emphasize is the fact that *prayer must come first,* that whatever duty has to be set aside for a time, prayer cannot be. Let us take this lesson from Hyde's life.

Our Saviour wept over Jerusalem, and this was one reason why Hyde had such influence over men—he followed the example of his Master and Paul and wept over men. Could we keep back the tears did we realise the terrible condition of men, the cost of their salvation, the sin of rejecting the message?

This comes from prayer, getting face to face with Christ—*the Crucified Christ,* and then going straight from the sacred, secret sanctuary of His presence to be face to face with a lost world, we would cry out with Jeremiah, "Oh, that my head were waters, and mine eyes a fountain of tears that I might weep day and night for those around us."

This is the Spirit of Christ that works in us—the spirit of prayer, of preaching, and of persuading men. Let us yield ourselves anew to the Spirit, and He will work this spirit into our lives.

Praying Hyde

PART III

A Master Fisher for Souls

BY R. M'CHEYNE PATERSON

PART III.

A Master Fisher for Souls.

Pleading with Tears.

J. N. was a Brahmin attending our mission school. As he grew up, the teaching of Christ attracted him, and he was the faithful scholar of one of our lady missionaries at Sunday school as well. When he left school and was beginning to earn his own living, he was drawn to confess publicly that Christ was his Saviour. He did this in the face of the bitterest opposition of a widowed mother and relations. Then they tried a more subtle plan: they began to please him. Their kindness won his heart—he went back home, and he was surrounded by young men who led him into drink. It must have been an inherited weakness with him. He fell, and denied his Lord. But, thank God, he was miserable, and went to see Mr. Hyde, who received him as did the father his prodigal son. The lad living with Mr. Hyde was won from his evil ways, and once again confessed faith in his Saviour: but what a trial he was when the drink demon would possess him! Again and again he stole Mr. Hyde's clothes, and sold them to satisfy his mad craving. I met Mr. Hyde about that time, and he said to me with a smile, "I may not get up to you to the hills this summer; the Father evidently desires me to spend my hot weather in the plains, for 'I have no warm clothes left!'" He took the "spoiling of his goods" cheerfully and thought they were a small price to pay in exchange for an immortal soul. He would point out how our Lord bore with Judas and others, how He never sent any away who were anxious to remain in His company, and so Hyde bore with this demon-possessed youth. In his sane moments the lad realised what a privilege was his to live with such a saint.

* * * * *

I was travelling in the train, and a Christian lady ticket-collecter met me at W——. She was full of a wonderful man she had seen. He was speaking to a lad seated in a train going to Lahore. The boy was loud and almost abusive. "I am tired of this sort of thing—I am going to my boon companions, and shall have a good time," he said. Then the gentleman he was speaking to leant forward and in a low tone begged him not to go away from him. He got back only a rude answer, and she, feeling angry and disgusted, left them. When she came back she saw the missionary still leaning into the carriage window, and she heard him beseeching the lad not to leave him. He was imploring him in Christ's Name, and she saw tears flowing down his cheeks as he reasoned with the head-strong lad. "Ah!" I exclaimed, "he knew the value of an immortal soul." In spite of all entreaties the lad took his own way, but to the very end that missionary was seen in deadly earnest trying to win that soul.

She lost sight of the missionary when the down train steamed out. (He went sadly to some dear friends in Gujerat alone).

Next day she saw the same lad coming back from Lahore. She said to him, "You have come back very soon again." He looked up with a pale face. "I am going back to him," he replied. "I have not been able to sleep all night—I could not forget his tears." And he came back a penitent. That missionary was John Hyde and that lad J.N.

I often feel that if souls could say the same of us, that we wept over them—our tears would bring them to a proper frame of mind. Our Lord's whole body shed tears—when "His sweat became as it were great drops of blood falling down upon the ground."

"Jesus wept." The Jews therefore said, "Behold, how He loved him!"

Soul-winners, can this be said of each one of us?

Grace Abounding!

Those interested in the case of the Brahmin lad mentioned in the previous memoir will be glad to hear that he afterwards paid me a visit. He seemed much chastened, and never before had he been so like his former self. He spoke of his aged mother as one who had to be considered, and the old narrow-minded Brahmin friend accompanying him said to me in a kind of stage-whisper: "He will be with you again whenever his mother dies." The lad heard it and smiled up assent with the old love in his eyes.

We talked long of John Hyde—whom he referred to as "up there," pointing Heavenward, and when I besought him once again to give up drink and become a teetotaller, he owned that he had not kept his promise. "With God's help you can." He agreed to that. Praise and pray on!

The same lad has visited me a second time, and we had a heart-to-heart talk about Mr. Hyde. He tells me that when he returned miserable from Lahore after running away from Mr. Hyde, he met me near the Mission school in the city and I told him Mr. Hyde was at our mission house.

He went there, and going to his room, found him praying. Mr. Hyde opened his eyes, saw him, took him into his arms and said, "I have just been praying that God would send you back to me, and see, He has answered me!"

When I asked him how he got to know Mr. Hyde so well, he told me a long story, the gist of which I set down just to show how this man of God used to win hearts for his Master. He saw Mr. Hyde at Moga railway station, went up to him, mentioned a fellow-missionary's name, and said that he had been baptised but had fallen back. "Why did you deny Christ?" Mr. Hyde asked. The lad began to make excuses, but Mr. Hyde took him with him, went into the third class waiting shed, and with two other Christians, the three knelt down and prayed with this lad —he kneeling among them even though a crowd gathered, and his relations came and saw him praying with the others. The lad says he does not remember exactly what Mr. Hyde said in prayer, but he prayed for him. Then the train came in, and he said goodbye to the lad, adding, "We will meet again in a week's time or so, God will arrange it."

All this made such an impression on the boy's heart that he took leave and set out to find Mr. Hyde. He at length heard that he was away inland at a Christian colony holding meetings. A Christian lad and he set out on foot for it, and after two days' travel arrived tired out. They were told that Mr. Hyde was in his room praying. He looked up, and seeing the Brahmin lad, took him in his arms in good Punjabi style, and then finding he was tired out, made him lie down and began to rub and press his swollen feet. The lad objected, but Mr. Hyde insisted upon waiting upon him and ministering to his wants with his own hands. He has told me of this with tears in his eyes, adding, "I often see him in my dreams before me as of old." "Remember, he is praying for you," I have reminded him.

That night while they were all eating dinner news came that the Indian pastor was taken suddenly ill, and at the same time his house had caught fire. Mr. Hyde ran with the others to help. While they fought the flames, he went to the pastor, and found him crying out in agony and, for fear of death, some unconfessed sin was evidently weighing on his conscience. Mr. Hyde talked and prayed with him, and then said, "I think it is God's will that you confess your sin in church before your congregation." The pastor agreed, and he was carried to church on his bed. Lying on it, with tears he declared that he had committed a great sin against God in that very church, and prayed for forgiveness. Then a great peace fell upon him, and all pain and sickness at once left him. Upon this some twenty members of the church were conscience-stricken, and confessed their sins, finding pardon and peace. They were joined by the others who had put out the fire, and the service lasted for an hour and a half, a great work for God beginning. Afterwards they all returned to their half-finished dinner.

The next day they left for a hill station where Mr. Hyde had received an urgent call to conduct evangelistic services. They travelled in the third class in the hot weather to the foot of the hills. They had only money for one pony and a coolie between them, so they got on the pony turn about. One night the Indian preacher was riding on ahead, when suddenly his pony stopped short, trembled in every limb, and advanced towards a great big cat, that seemed to fascinate the poor beast with its eyes. Then the preacher felt a big body whiz through the air and land just behind him; the pony, recovering itself, dashed away up the road and leaped a ditch at the side in its terror, leaving the baffled tiger standing on the roadside. It must have slunk away, for when Mr. Hyde passed there was no sign of the animal. When they came near the bungalow they were met by the preacher in a great panic, along with a number of men who had gone back with sticks to see what had happened to Mr. Hyde. He made them go back to the place where the tiger had made his spring. In the moonlight they saw the marks of its paws on the dust of the roadside; but the animal had gone. They heard that it had killed people and many bullocks. They remained a week in that hill station, and held daily services for Christians. A real work of grace began there, and this lad, too, was convicted of the sin of denying his Lord, and, making confession, was again received into fellowship. On their return journey they each had a pony. "So they went like beggars and returned like kings!"

The lad laughed and said, "Yes, and a missionary lent me his own pony to ride back on because one of the Christian workers had said to me, 'Why did you come and increase the expenses?' and I had burst into tears at this rebuke."

Perhaps friends will join me in prayer about this lad also. It is not for nothing that God has sent him back to me and he is sitting by my side as I write.

The Secret of Hyde's Power with God and with Men—"Giving Thanks in Everything!"

This is God's command to those who would be full of the Holy Spirit, and no one I have ever known obeyed this command more faithfully than John Hyde. It was one great source of his joy and therefore of his attractive power. Again and again he would declare that if we want to know why trials are sent us, let us begin by thanking God for them, and we will doubtless soon see why they have been sent. We had among ourselves a phrase, "Praising God through shut teeth," that meant praising God in the face of the greatest troubles and darkest hours of life. This we can always do, for we can never doubt that He is our Father in Heaven, and so all must be well for us at all times and in all circumstances.

He used to tell of a remarkable experience he had. He and his catechists were all itinerating together in his district. They had arrived at a village, and as it was the hot weather, they had to rise early to go out preaching. This morning John awoke with one of his worst headaches; it was so painful that he could not lift his head from his pillow. Yet he could look up to his Heavenly Father and thank Him for the love that had permitted that headache! His evangelists carried his bed out to a shady place and then went away to preach at his express desire. Now in that village, work among the womenfolk was at a standstill. Some of the men had learnt of Christ and confessed Him in baptism; but their wives had never come forward. When spoken to they would always make the excuse that they had never consulted each other, so that all of them might be baptised together. These women heard that the Padri Sahib was not well, and in a body went to commiserate with him. He spoke to them of the claims of Christ, which they at once admitted. Yes, they believed He had died for them, sinners. John asked them why they had not confessed Him before men. They said they had not talked the matter over among themselves. He said there was no time like the present, let them do so now. To this they agreed, and after some discussion they all declared that it was plain to them that they ought to be baptised. To the great joy of their husbands and the evangelists this was done, and John Hyde saw why the headache had been sent. He was enabled to thank God then with understanding. He always declared this experience was a valuable lesson to him and enabled him to thank God "for all things" "at all times."

Now this became no mechanical habit on his part, but a deep-rooted principle of his life founded on experience of God's marvellous love. The deeper our sense of that love, the more we will be able to praise and thank Him. How John Hyde used to agonise in prayer for believers that they might know the love of God! In this matter he was strictly in the Apostolic Succession—a Succession for all missionaries, both men and women.

Mr. Hyde had a wonderful experience, to which he owed, I believe, his power with God, and therefore with man. He used to speak of it as one of the most direct and solemn lessons God had ever taught him. He was up in the hills resting for a short time. He had been burdened about the spiritual condition of a certain pastor, and he resolved to spend time in definite intercession for him. Entering into his "inner chamber," he began pouring out his heart to his Heavenly Father concerning that brother somewhat as follows:

"O God! Thou knowest that brother how—" "cold" he was going to say, when suddenly a Hand seemed to be laid on his lips, and a Voice said to him in stern reproach, "He that toucheth him, toucheth the apple of Mine eye." A great horror came over him. He had been guilty before God of "accusing the brethren." He had been "judging" his brother. He felt rebuked and humbled before God. It was he himself who first needed putting right. He confessed this sin. He claimed the precious Blood of Christ that cleanseth from all sin! "Whatsoever things are lovely . . . if there be any virtue, if there be any praise, think on these things." Then he cried out, "Father, show me what things are lovely and of good report in my brother's life." Like a flash he remembered how that brother had given up all for Christ, enduring much suffering from relations whom he had given up. He was reminded of his years of hard work, of the tact with which he managed his difficult congregation, of the many quarrels he had healed, of what a model husband he was. One thing after another rose up before him and so all his prayer season was spent in praise for his brother instead of in prayer.

He could not recall a single petition, nothing but thanksgiving! God was opening His servant's eyes to the highest of ministries, that of praise.

Mark the result also on that brother's life! When Mr. Hyde went down to the plains, he found that just then the brother had received a great spiritual uplift. While he was praising, God was blessing. *A wonderful Divine Law*, the law of a Father's love. While we bless God for any child of His, He delights to bless that one!

This was the secret of John Hyde's power with God. *He saw the good* in God's little ones, and so was able to appreciate God's work of grace in that heart. Hence he supplied the Heavenly atmosphere of praise in which God's love was free to work in all its fulness.

This, too, was what gave him power with men. *We are attracted to those who appreciate us.* All our powers expand in their presence, and we are with them at our best. Hence they call out all that is good in us, and we feel uplifted when with them.

To such souls we turn as naturally as the flowers to the sun, and our hearts expand and bloom out with a fragrance that surprises even ourselves.

Now this is a law that holds good especially with children, and with those who are yet young in the Christian life. The more mature God's people are the less they depend on man's approbation or censure, but not so when they are children. Remember, too, our Lord's solemn warning against casting a stumbling block in the way of any of His little ones! When we look at their faults, we shrivel up their energies, they are at their worst. In a word, *we encourage their faults by thinking about them.*

Let us remember above all else that God's people on this earth are in the making. This is His workshop and souls are being fashioned and formed in it. The final polishing touches we will not receive in the present life, but when this body of our humiliation has been transformed. Suppose you go into a carpenter's shop and begin to find fault with his unfinished chairs and tables! You say, "How rough this is! What an ugly corner that is!" The carpenter will doubtless get angry and say, "Bear in mind that I am still making these things. They are not yet finished. Come and see the pattern after which they are being fashioned. See, this is what they will yet be like when I have done with them." He shows you beautiful chairs and tables—shining, perfectly formed, polished to perfection! Is the carpenter not right? Is the critic not in the wrong? The one looks at the things that are lovely and eternal. The other at those which are unlovely and, thank God, fleeting.

Would you have power with God and man for the upbuilding of the Indian Church—of any Church? Follow the method of the Carpenter of Nazareth who never broke the bruised reed, who never quenched the smoking wick, no matter how much smoke it was giving out. He turned His eyes to the light of God, there burning dimly, and by so doing blew it into a flame till erring disciples became the Light of the World. This is the way of Love and of Eternal Hope. The other is the way of sense and of present fact and failure—all of which are fleeting—none of which is the Eternal Truth in Eternal Love.

I never met any man whose very presence seemed to help the weak to become strong, the sinful to repent, the erring to walk aright so much as John Hyde. The secret of his success in building up the people of God lay in this method of *looking for all the good in men* and making it so to expand that the evil was driven out for want of room. Then should we shut our eyes to the faults of all? Should we never reprove sin? Turn to our Lord. Did He not do so at times? Yes, to the impenitent—to those who opposed Him and would not come to Him for help. Just because He was in the habit of looking at all that was good—for that very reason He was able to reprove with all the greater power. No one could do so more severely than our Lord just because He loved much and sympathised so much with all that was good in men.

One Cause of His Success

It will be a comfort to many when they hear that Mr. John Hyde was not naturally a bright and happy man. On the contrary, he was in himself inclined to be morose, retiring, shy, and silent. Yet he became one of the most joyous souls I have ever met.

He was very fond of Isaiah 61. 3, where that wonderful exchange is effected by our Lord. He will give us His own "Beauty," His own "Oil of Joy," and His own "Garment of Praise" if we hand over to Him our ashes (what is our past life but "ashes"?), our mourning and our spirit of heaviness. So he received our Lord's double gift of joy (John 15. 11), freely from his Master's hand, and then would burst out into joyful praise. For no one can be filled with the Divine joy and not sing His praise. As we joy in God we soar up into His immediate presence, and it is only in song that our joy finds vent. As well expect the soaring lark to keep silent as expect the joyous saint not to sing God's praise.

In this matter of praise Mr. Hyde used to tell how "a little child shall lead them." He was taught again and again that joyful praise is the Divine method for catching men alive.

One day he was in a country cart travelling to a distant village. His faithful Punjabi evangelist was with him—one who was transformed through contact with John Hyde. Two of the evangelist's little children were in the cart. The elders were speaking sadly about the village—how long the Gospel had been preached there and how little interest had been aroused among its people. The children had no such sad thoughts; they were so happy that they sang, and went on singing psalms and hymns one after the other. This was infectious, and the two men were constrained to join them, and they, too, were so carried away with the spirit of praise that they all continued singing till they came to that village. Imagine their amazement when they found the people full of real interest and zealous to confess Christ and follow Him. Before they left over a dozen showed such a living faith in their Lord and Saviour that Mr. Hyde felt he dared not refuse them baptism then and there. Thus was the first Gospel triumph in that village heralded and brought about, he was confident, by the spirit of praise which the children had evinced.

Another time they had a more marked experience. He, with a party of his evangelists, was encamped in a certain village where the work had been carried on for thirty years. The farm servants had for years been putting off the question of deciding for Christ. They were now in the habit of saying, "Not now during the harvest, but afterwards when it is over." So, alas! every year it had ended with:

> "The harvest is past, the summer ended, and we are not saved." (Jer. 8. 20.)

This mission party were so disheartened by their previous experiences that on this occasion they had made up their minds to leave early next morning. That night some one suggested they should all go into the village and sing the Gospel in it. This they did, and they were so carried away that they sang on and on till after midnight. Next morning they were preparing to leave when a young man came running from the village. He begged them not to go away, for the Panchayat (council) had been called and was meeting even now. No one had gone to work that morning; they were considering whether they should not at once decide for Christ and confess Him before all men. They gladly waited, and presently the same young man came running back with the welcome news that they had all decided to serve Christ. Mr. Hyde found some fifteen men—mostly the heads of families—quite prepared for baptism, and with an overflowing heart he baptised them before all. After the service that same young man who had brought the message—a new convert—said to Mr. Hyde, "This is the result of your singing last night.

"You remember how we sang:

> 'Lift up your heads, O ye gates,
> And let the King of Glory enter in!'

"Has He not entered in this morning?" No one had noticed till then the connection between the song of triumph of the night before and the reality of that triumph of the next morning until they learnt it from this babe in Christ. Yes, verily,

> "Out of the mouths of babes and sucklings
> Thou hast perfected praise."

In fact, Mr. Hyde used to say that at any time when he noticed few souls being led by him to Christ, he invariably found *it was all due to his lack of the spirit of praise.* He would then confess his sin, ask pardon, and take the Garment of Praise for the spirit of heaviness. His experience then invariably was that Christ would again draw souls to Himself through him. Now the reason for this is plain. No fisher can possibly throw his line lightly when he is dull and sad. It is only the bright and joyous soul that can win souls to Christ. Notice how St. Paul connects these two in Philippians 4. He is speaking of his fellow-labourers or fellow-fishers and of their success in the work. Then he goes on as if to give the reason for this success and how it may be continued:

"Rejoice in the Lord always,
And again I say unto you rejoice."

A Second Cause of his Success

This was his wonderful love for souls. It overpowered all else, making him forget everything but that soul with whom God had brought him into contact. He would go on past his railway station as far as the man with whom he was in touch who was travelling, in order to talk to him the "Words of Life." This was irritating at times, especially once when he was almost ordered to attend an important business meeting of his mission. He met an Indian in the train when travelling to that same meeting, fell into conversation with him about Christ, and continued the train journey with him that he might tell him more of the Saviour of the world. This made him late for that meeting, no doubt to the annoyance of even his best friends, but John Hyde's mind was at peace. He had bought up his opportunity (Eph. 6. 16), paying a heavy price for it, perhaps, and had faithfully held Christ up to a soul that had need of Him. That was sufficient motive and reward for John Hyde. It must be said his mission at last saw his gifts, and this special work to which he seemed more and more drawn as he grew older, and set him free for it. One of his old evangelists, who shared his village mud house with John Hyde for some time, once told me with tears of regret in his eyes of his great love for souls. He said Mr. Hyde was always giving away his clothes, anything he had, to those who came to see him about the things of God. "If by any means I may win some" seems to have been his life's aim.

One cold winter night Mr. Hyde tapped at the door of this evangelist's room. It was late, and he did not want to open. So Mr. Hyde called out his name, and said, "Can you lend me a sheet for the night?" "Where are your own blankets?" was the angry retort through the still closed door. "Oh, yes! that drunken sot that was with you has gone off with them. He will sell them, get drink, and make a beast of himself. Do you know that you put us all about by doing things like this and then shivering yourself in the cold?" He owned with remorse how impertinent he had been, and the tears came to his big black eyes as he asked me if I could imagine all the answer Mr. Hyde gave him. He called him by his name, and said, "Ah, J——! J——! If the prodigal had come back to you, you would have taken a stick to him!"

This same evangelist told of another experience. It was in the days when souls were being gathered in. They were at times assured how many would be granted them. That morning after prayer it was ten souls. They then set out away among the Punjab villages in a country cart. The road lay along a river bank, dangerous at night. They reached that village. They sang, they preached, then sang again and preached. The day wore on. Not a sign even of one soul being interested. They became hungry and thirsty. No man gave unto them. Then the two Indian evangelists became impatient to get home to food and rest. But John Hyde would not move. He was waiting for those ten. At last near a common cottage they asked for a drink. The man offered them milk and water. They went into his humble house and were refreshed. Then as they talked he showed most intelligent knowledge of Jesus Christ. Yes, he had entertained them in His Name. Would the family not allow Jesus to enter and take possession of their home? The father replied they had been thinking of this. Then why not now? He agreed, and called his wife and children. They certainly realised what they were doing, and there and then made up their minds to take their stand at once on the Lord's side.

One can picture how tenderly John Hyde received them into God's family in the name of the Father, and the Son, and the Holy Spirit. Yes, all were baptised, *nine* altogether. It was now getting dark, the short cold-weather day was wearing to an end rapidly. Now at any rate they could depart, so thought the two evangelists, before the darkness made their return journey dangerous. The father began to urge it, too. Unwillingly John Hyde left that home. The cart was sent for by one, the other hastened John Hyde's steps towards it. When it came they tried to get him to climb in. But no, his eyes were fixed pleadingly on this evangelist. "What about that *one*?" he asked, longingly. Surely that cry from a true shepherd's heart found a response! He hardened his face, and said something about their wives and children being anxious for them at home. But John Hyde stood there waiting, waiting for that tenth soul. He knew that the Good Shepherd was Himself searching for that one still outside the Fold. The two evangelists told me afterwards with shame how they urged John Hyde to come away from that village, and how the same cry always broke from his lips "What about that one?"

By and by the father of the family came up wondering about this delay—why had the Padre Sahib waited so long? John Hyde told him about the one sheep still wanting. "Why there he is," cried the father, "my nephew whom I have adopted. He has been living with the rest of us: but has been out playing." He brought the lad forward, a bright intelligent boy. Mr. Hyde asked him of his faith. The boy answered very clearly and intelligently. There could be no doubt about him. So he, too, was brought into the fold. "That is the ten," said John Hyde with a weary sigh of heart's ease as he climbed up to his seat. They were kept safe along that dangerous road in the darkness and arrived home tired but content. That is the "rest of soul" our Lord Jesus gives to His faithful earnest under-shepherds. Yes, and that is the rest of soul they give Him, too, for in their passion and longing for the lost, He sees of the travail of his soul and is satisfied.

Lord teach us at whatever cost to satisfy Thy great heart of love, broken over wandering sheep. So shall we apply balm and healing to that Heart. So shall we bind up Thy wounds and give Thee the joy that was set before Thee. May we realise that the angels envy us such service! They cannot render it unto Thee. Only pardoned sinners can, by bringing others into the circle of Thy pardoning Love.

Lord show us that this passion for souls cannot be worked up by any efforts of our own. It comes forth from Thy bleeding heart, O Thou Lamb upon the Throne, Who art still giving forth Thy glorified Life for us, "He ever liveth to make intercession for us." We praise Thee O Lamb of God that Thou madest known Thy Father's Name and wilt make it known, "That the love, wherewith Thou, O Father, lovedst me may be in them and I in them."

His Child-like Obedience

Not a day did I pass in John Hyde's company but his simple obedience surprised me and led me to see what a real son he was, and how much his Heavenly Father's will guided his life. Let me mention one such instance. Once at the Sialkot Convention, which was so inspired by his prayers in those old days, the Committee, in order to lay stress on the message instead of on its messengers, did not announce the names of the speakers. John Hyde was suddenly asked to speak at the evening meeting. Somehow it got noised abroad and many were saying "Mr. Hyde will speak to-night!" The meeting was very full and expectant, especially as a great friend of his was in the chair in place of the usual chairman. Just before the speaker's prayer meeting this friend was asked what Psalm should be sung. The subject of our Lord's sufferings being much on his heart, he suggested the 22nd Psalm. Imagine his surprise when the leader of song announced that they would sing the 22nd Psalm at Mr. Hyde's request. It was supposed they had talked it over together. There was much prayer, the praise was fervent; but Mr. Hyde was sitting down on the platform behind the pulpit deep in prayer. As he did not move, the chairman read Zechariah 13, commenting at some length on that question and answer, "What are those wounds between thine hands?" Then he shall answer, "Those with which I was wounded in the house of my friends." He spoke of the loneliness of Christ in His sufferings, no one knowing about His sorrows and pointed out that only three disciples even entered Gethsemane with our Lord; the other eight were left outside; those three, alas, were full of sleep, so much so that Peter referring to this with a certain guilty conscience speaks of himself as only a "witness of the sufferings of Christ, who am also a partaker of the glory that shall be revealed." He was not yet a partaker of these sufferings. So is it to-day; the majority of Christians know nothing of Gethsemane. At the best a few are "witnesses" only of His sufferings. Hence the world is not won for Christ, nor will it be until His people as a whole become fellow-partakers of His sufferings.

All this time John Hyde was lost in prayer. After this the chairman during another singing laid his hands on his shoulder and said with a friendly squeeze, "If God has a message, for you to give, will you give it now?"

As John did not move, the late John Forman, then chairman of the Convention, said to his brother in the chair, "Is he going to speak?" "I have asked him," was the reply, "You ask him, too, if you are led to do it." Presently as the singing stopped he said, "May I give two messages God has laid on my heart?" He did so, and the meeting proceeded to its close after which, there was a very earnest after-meeting and much prayer by those present. During that time John Hyde went away to the Prayer Room without addressing a word to the meeting. The people were thus taught to attend to God's message and not to the messenger.

Some time afterwards I asked him about that matter. He told me that he felt full of a subject, "The Glory of Christ's Kingdom." When however, the chairman laid his hand on his shoulder, he seemed as if he pressed John down. This thought was enforced by his words, "If you have a message from God." John began to doubt if God wanted him to give this message then, and so of course, waited on God in prayer and never had His direct leading to speak to that meeting!

Only a man very closely in touch with his Heavenly Father would have been quick enough to follow this leading and only one whose supreme wish was to please God and not his fellow-men would have been brave enough to keep silence in the circumstances.

A friend, afterwards speaking of the Revival, said to me: "We ought to have emphasised the lesson of absolute obedience more than we did. I believe it was want of obedience that grieved the Holy Spirit and stopped that Revival."

I could not but agree with him, at the same time telling him this incident to show that one of the leaders in that Revival at least could not be accused of the sin of disobedience.

Honouring the Holy Spirit.

All know how loyally John Hyde supported the Sialkot Convention. It was really his addresses that led to the great blessing in that first Convention of 1904. This Convention was attended largely by missionaries especially those in the vicinity; and it was a time when God met His own people: when "self" was unveiled: when God called His own to a deeper consecration: when the Holy Spirit convicted of sin and led to many changed lives. In fact, it was there that the heart-surrender of the leaders took place which led to the Revival of 1905. Mr. Hyde's addresses on the Holy Spirit were much used of God to this great end.

This Convention in the summer of 1904 owed much also to the Punjab Prayer Union, begun by a few souls (about April, 1904) on whom the burden of united prayer for Revival had been heavily laid. Needless to say, one of the moving spirits of this union was John Hyde. All its members were greatly inspired by his habits of prayer—and by his whole life of intercession. Most particularly did they value and benefit by his presence at the annual meetings of the Union. His addresses there appealed to many hearts, and the conversation he had with them led to lives of joy and service such as had never been dreamt of before.

Who can forget that memorable annual meeting of the Punjab Prayer Union in the spring of 1905? It was a time when all felt the great burden of the Indian Church, and her need of revival, so very keenly as to be inexpressible in words. This was mainly due to the teaching of John Hyde and those like him in regard to "the fellowship of Christ's sufferings." There was a general breakdown of all hearts when this subject was talked and prayed about. To many the Lamb of God appeared with His wounded hands and side, and showed them how His heart was still being made to bleed by His children when they were not fully consecrated to Him, and when they were not filled to overflowing with His Spirit. Little wonder that the Convention of 1905 touched so deeply the life of the Punjab Church! Here again John Hyde was the moving spirit of the whole Convention. It seemed as if the mantle of his second great spiritual teacher (the first was Mr. Ullmann)—D. Lytle of the American United Presbyterian Mission—had descended upon him. The burden of Mr. Lytle's later teaching had been that self-support could only be looked for on the old Apostolic lines—when the baptism of the Holy Spirit and then the constant infilling of the Holy Spirit, received its true place in the heart and life of the Christian community. Then self-supporting congregations would spring up everywhere as a natural consequence. Mr. Lytle loved to point out that almost all the Apostolic congregations over forty in number were self-supporting and also self-propagating simply because they put first things first, and never rested till they had received the Baptism, and then the infilling of the Holy Spirit for every new service.

This was the burden of John Hyde's addresses at the Sialkot Convention of 1905. What a thrilling message he delivered! How plainly he showed that the Holy Spirit was the One True Witness—to be put first and foremost by all Christians—so that they might also give their witness in His strength and by His help. When he addressed pastors, asking them who was first and foremost in their pulpits—

they themselves, or the Divine Teacher and Guide into all the truth—I don't think there was a single preacher who was not convicted of this sin.

Then he went right through the Life of Christ—showing how all the mysterious events of that life were performed by means of the Holy Spirit—our Lord's Birth, His Baptism, His preaching, His miracles, His Sacrifice, His Resurrection, the Holy Spirit was witness of each event, so He alone is the true witness. When John Hyde called upon all to see to it that this Divine Witness was depended on to teach all inquiring souls the meaning and the mystery of each event, few hearts were unmoved. And then afterwards when John Hyde intimated that he had no other message to give, the chairman was led to leave each meeting to the guidance of the Holy Spirit—surely that was the direct result of this teaching! What else could result but that the Divine Spirit, given His true place, should move all hearts, break them down, melt them into confession and tears, and so begin the first great Revival in the Punjab?

In the Convention of 1904, missionaries were much blessed. It was then that one leader brought things to a crisis by saying: "Either we missionaries receive power from on high now, or else let us all take the first steamer home, for we are otherwise unfit for this task." In the 1905 Convention our Pastors and elders were laid hold of largely through Mr. Hyde's teaching and perfect obedience. In the Convention of 1906 the blessing extended to Christians generally and reached outside congregations all over Northern India.

Memories of the First Annual Meeting of the Punjab Prayer Union.

At the first meeting in the spring of 1905 we were kept for days in His presence and oh, how He revealed "self" by revealing Christ and Him crucified. It seemed as if He bowed us lower and still lower in the white light of His holiness—showing more and more of our blackness and blankness and more and more of His exceeding fulness of love. John Hyde was most impressed by the experience of the other three with him alone in a little chamber. To that little band Jesus was revealed in a new way suffering and dying for the sake of India, His love seemed to flow out of His broken heart in unceasing streams, North and South, and East and West. "You, before whose very eyes was held up a picture of Jesus Christ on the Cross" (Gal. 3. 1) (Conybeare & Howson), or "You to whom Jesus Christ has been vividly portrayed as on the Cross" (Weymouth). Yes, He was so revealed to us four that afternoon.

As in that famous passage of Zechariah 12. 10 we mourned for Him and were in bitterness for Him when we looked on Him Whom we had pierced. But how those tears were changed into a holy joy when we realised that India was now Christ's—as the whole world, too, is—because He had bought it unto His Father "by His Blood." Yes, that was John Hyde's place of "emptying"—the Cross. There God lays His emphasis on our being empty, for it is only the want of room that hinders all the wealth of grace in Christ from flooding our hearts continuously so that from within them may flow those "rivers of living water" promised by our Lord in regard to every believing child of His. How that emphasis was laid upon the "emptying" again and again by John Hyde to the very end of his life we realised when we heard him speak of that deep subject in 2 Kings 3: "Thus saith Jehovah," "Make this valley full of trenches." Aye, only valleys are fertile and glorify God aright! So hills must be made low. Yet even these valleys must be made full of trenches. We must go deeper and still deeper down with our Lord into His grave—for He was crucified, dead, and buried. The old self has to be buried—put out of sight that it no more offend one of God's little ones or come between the Living Saviour and seeking souls. Oh, that we would learn Martha's lesson and not keep the dead in their graves by coming between them and the Life-Giving One even as she did.

No wonder John Hyde so definitely covenanted

with his Lord that if at any time he came between a soul and its Saviour, He would put him aside, stop him and show him his sin even as He did to Martha and others! That illustration of a tree burying itself deeper into the ground and so growing *upward* the more it went down was constantly used in those early days. "In days to come Jacob (the old man), shall take root; Israel (the new man), shall blossom and bud; and *they* (both the old man by dying more and more and the new man by so blossoming more and more), shall fill the face of the world with fruit" (Isa. 27. 6). This is repeated for our instruction, "And the remnant that is escaped of the house of Judah shall *again take root downward and bear fruit upward*" (Isa. 37. 31).

Empty Vessels not a Few

John was very fond of the next chapter (2 Kings 4), and the "even empty vessels . . . not a few." How eagerly he would point out that the empty vessels failed first and it was only the want of empty vessels that stopped the flowing of the oil; it is always we who are to blame when the Spirit's work ceases, never He. He dwelt much on how our Lord emptied Himself. He was constantly doing it: always giving up even from the age of twelve, yea, before that when He became man, yea, even before that when He became the Creative Word carrying out in Creation the Father's will and saying, "Let there be light." Yea, even before this when in eternity He yielded to the Father's plan of redemption, and so was "the Lamb slain before the foundation of the world."

See how our Lord gave up His own privacy for His unsympathetic disciples in John 1! How He gave up home, and then friends, rest, and comfort. How He gave up His own mother at last and life itself! What else could our Lord have given up that He did not give up as He hung despised and rejected of men—giving up honour itself—on the Cross? This entering more and more deeply into the death of our Lord was the secret of John Hyde's growth in every spiritual grace and very especially in his passion for souls. Let me tell of an experience I had with him in that same church whose pastor he wanted to pray for and ended by praising for and with such a glorious result. They arranged for a series of meetings for some days. I was invited to be the preacher. John was as usual out of sight—in the prayer room. His face was drawn and thin—it was apparently a hard fight. I never encountered a blacker wall of indifference and stolid content. Night after night the atmosphere remained cold and dead. Poor John seemed to shrivel up more and more. The burden on him was awful! I just fancy I see that black cold night we had to face, and to this day it fills my soul with horror as of darkness out of the bottomless pit. Yet all that should have filled my soul with the joy of victory, for *the greater Satan's efforts the more certain it is that His conqueror will tread him under His feet.* Oh, struggling saints of God! The harder the struggle, the more hope should possess your souls, for Satan only fights hardest where he is most afraid of defeat. So the more he seems to prevail, the more glorious the victory at hand!

At length the very last night of those meetings came. The message was given with tears—not another eye was wet—not a heart touched. John was as usual in the "inner chamber," his face buried on the floor in agony of supplication. We all knew where he was and what doing. Just after the address our aged friend and chief elder (now with John—yea, rather with his Master—in glory), came forward and asked in a low voice permission to speak. Of course it was gladly granted. He turned to the audience and said, "Brethren, you may have noticed that I have been very seldom at these meetings. The reason is that God has had a controversy with me. You all know that a famous Persian carpet is for sale in this station. Well, I had made up my mind to buy it, and thought that if it went cheap I would keep it for my own drawing-room; but if it went dear it could be put in my office and Government would pay for it (he was a distinguished Government servant). Every time I came to these meetings that carpet started up before my eyes and kept me from getting my blessing. Now I have resolved that if that carpet sells dear I'll have it for myself, but if it sells cheap it will go into my office." Then he cried aloud in agony, "Oh, brethren, it is I, your chief elder, who has been standing between your souls and blessing! I have put that stumbling-block in your way! I confess it with shame. God forgive me for this great sin I have committed against you His people as well as against Him!"

How marvellously He showed His forgiveness! How He there and then "cleansed from all unrighteousness!" All were touched; not a dry eye to be seen there. Tears flowing to the right and left. The tense silence was broken by another elder. "Brethren, our friend is not the only one who has been preventing blessing from this congregation. I have been a greater sinner than all. I have for years been quarrelling with my brother elder"—and he named the man with whom he had for long had deep never-dying enmity—"I have been telling lies about him." There was a movement away on the opposite side of the church. A man rose, his face working. "Brother, I have been a bigger sinner than you about this. Only to-day I have been telling lies about you. I pray you to forgive me, for God has graciously heard my cry for pardon and forgiven me." Then the two moved towards one another, and there in the church these life-long enemies embraced each other as brothers in Christ.

What followed no pen can describe. "There is joy in the presence of the angels of God over one sinner that repenteth." What a joy when so many were repenting. That congregation, more divided perhaps than even the church at Corinth, though, thank God, not so full of glaring sins (yet St. Paul can thank God for the grace and gifts that *had* been given unto a Church that sank so low)—that congregation was united as one family in Christ that night. On all sides old enemies were becoming friends. The Holy Spirit was convicting all of sin and leading to this great tenderness and forgiveness of the past. I heard one sister say to another, "You remember that cock you lost and you blamed me for its disappearance? Yes, I *did* kill it. I'll send you over two hens in its place" (a fourfold requittal).

"No, no," says the other. "I ought not to have allowed it into your garden to destroy your plants," or some such excuse. A lad caught me by the feet—he was kneeling before me weeping. "Padre Sahib, forgive me; for Christ's sake, forgive me." "My boy, I have never seen you before." "I know that, but during all the meetings I have been speaking against them." "God has forgiven you, my son. How can I do otherwise?"

And John Hyde? He was seeing of the travail of Christ's soul and ours, being satisfied. But he was out of sight that all the glory might be to God alone. No tears are ever in vain. *It is only when His people travail in pain that souls are born again.* No soul is born without such birth-pangs. And those pangs are temporary—fleeting, for they give place to joy when the soul enters the Kingdom. But there are other pangs—life-long—not passing away—nay, ever becoming deeper and deeper, even that Third baptism to which our Lord looked forward and longed that it were over!

"I came to cast fire upon the earth."
"And what is my desire?"
"Oh, that it were even now kindled!"
"But I have a baptism to be baptised with."
"And how am I straitened till it be accomplished."

St. Paul speaks of the same baptism when he says "My little children of whom *I am again in travail* till Christ be formed in you!" He thus shows that there is a second and continuous agony which will become greater and deeper, "till Christ is formed in His people." Therein is the glorious fellowship of Christ's sufferings—a fellowship, however, which continues unto "His patience and unto His *Kingdom,*" as well, thank God! For how could we expect to endure daily such life-long suffering unless His patience was our treasure-house to draw upon.

Hyde as an Intercessor

Let us remember that it is our Great High Priest alone who made John Hyde an intercessor like Himself. No, not equal to Himself, for "He ever liveth to make intercession for us." The same Christ can fill each one of us with His own prayer life so that it becomes as natural for us to pray as it is for us to breathe. We don't need to give up our daily duties to be such intercessors. What if those very duties which once were stumbling-block in the way of prayer can be transformed by Christ's Holy Spirit into stepping-stones, enabling us to pray all the more! What if a new atmosphere of prayer can be breathed into us and into our daily work by Him who still baptiseth in the Holy Ghost and in fire! What if we have two Divine Intercessors—the One within us praying according to the will of God and so teaching us how to pray as we ought, and how to go on praying and not faint; the other presenting our prayers faultless before the Throne and ensuring answers "exceeding abundantly above all that we can ask or think."

What if we have all the soul-passion of Jesus Christ our glorified Lord to draw upon at our every hour of need! What if His love is ours to make use of moment by moment!

"Righteous Father . . . I have declared unto them Thy Name (Father) and will declare it (Blessed

Promise!) that the love wherewith Thou hast loved Me may be in them (what a wealth for us!) and I in them." What a comfort His presence is, for He is the source of all we daily and hourly need—all the wisdom and power and grace and longsuffering and gentleness and joy and peace and hope, and above all, love! All are hidden in Him—hidden from the world, but seen by the eye of faith and open to the hand of faith to take out and make use of moment by moment. "Oh, but I so often forget this!" We at times cry. Well, there is a Divine Remembrancer —sent to remind us of the things of Christ—"to bring them to our remembrance!" *"What more could I have done for thee,"* saith our God and Father, *"that I have not done?"* This dependence on Christ and His Spirit was the secret of John Hyde's success in everything—especially in the prayer life. This is the open secret of every saint of God! "My strength blossoms out to perfection in weakness" is His word. So "when I am weak, I am strong"—strong with Divine strength. The more we grow in grace, the more dependent we become! Never let us forget this glorious fact, and then we will be able to thank God for our *bad* memories, for our *weak* bodies—"for everything," and in that sacrifice of praise shall be His delight, and also our own. So this fruit shall fill the whole earth!

Praying Hyde

PART IV

Extracts from his Letters

PART IV.

Letters of John Hyde

Letters to His College Magazine

"LAST year (1893) until June 1st, I was at my station studying Hindustani, then I went to the Himalayas for three weeks, and was there again a week later; saw many missionaries and enjoyed it. The rest of the time till November 15th I spent in Dehra Dun. I was studying there under Mr. Ullman, one of our missionaries sent out some 55 years ago by Mr. Gossur of Berlin. He is a fine teacher, and his spiritual influence was most helpful to me: a distinct blessing came to me there after months of seeking. The Blood of Jesus now has to me a power not realised before. Most of the winter and spring until to-day was spent among the villages with Indian preachers. Yesterday eight low-caste persons were baptised at one of the villages. It seems a work of God in which man, even as an instrument, was used in a very small degree. Pray for us. I learn to speak the language very, very slowly: can talk only a little in public or in conversation. For my classmates I pray constantly. Will not some of you come out this year? The labourers are few—so few."

The following note will be of interest: "Hyde was an old friend of mine in the Punjab days, and I well remember his sending in his resignation to the Synod in despair of getting the language owing to his deafness. With his letter came a petition from his village people begging the Synod *not* to accept the resignation on the plea: '*If he never speaks the language of our lips. he speaks the language of our hearts.*' And so he stayed, to become one of the best linguists in the Mission."

Letter to Seminary Magazine

We can see in his letters to his Seminary Magazine the burdens that began to weigh heavily upon him even then. This is how he writes at the close of the year 1895—what a change has come over the Punjab since.

"I am associated with Mr. Martin of Lahore, and work with him in both districts—Lahore and Ferozepore. This work lies among the countless villages and towns, containing probably 1,200,000 people, but especially among the low castes, whose numbers I think will reach about 200,000. They form the despised serf element of almost all villages, and are degraded enough to eat the flesh of animals that die of themselves. In the Lahore district among them are some 300 or 400 Christians in nine or ten villages. In this district a handful of them live in some three villages who have been baptised within the year that ends to-day (1895). To minister to these and to extend the work to other villages is our employment. I know the work here in Lauke best, so will try to picture it to you. The low-caste Christian teacher here and a man of a near village discussed together for some time last summer, with no result. Our teacher gave him a copy of the New Testament, for, better than most, he could read. He told me the other day that when he came to the words, 'Heaven and earth shall pass away, but My Words shall not pass away,' then he was convinced. Now he himself is one of our teachers. Thus we have been given a teacher. God gave us a little revival season here for some two or three weeks in January. In these same meetings I remember how one low-caste man's face and mind seemed to take in the word—literally to drink it in, and I was given such simpleness and clearness of expression that I wonder at it yet.

"At our early morning prayer meetings during those weeks we all prayed short prayers, and men learned to pray there. This will let you see a little of the work that was most encouraging. We would like to see similar things in each of the villages where there are Christians. Another picture is this. We have been here again for a month. Now is the persecution time. The villagers who are not Christians, those of the higher castes, have tried to stop our water-carriers from bringing us water, have stolen from us, and I understand have threatened to pull down our tents, all apparently to get us away. They have succeeded in taking the house our teacher occupied, so we have no place for a teacher here. Last Saturday night one of the Christians was beaten, and they threaten them all with such suffering that these are times of trouble and trial of faith. I have been much at the Throne—I have needed to go for myself, too—but it is a Throne of Grace.

"While I have already occupied more than my share of space, it will let you into the work here better, perhaps, than any other way. As for myself, may I say humbly that since coming to India God has given me an understanding with Himself. We have come to understand each other. He is apparently ready to bless the missionaries, workers, Christians and non-Christians, especially the low-castes. Pray in faith for immediate blessings in India. Wilder has been among us some of the past year. He was in Lahore in February, and we hear that Dr. Ewing, the President of our College there, has received the Pentecostal gift, and that others have entered in. Praise the Lord!"

His letter to his college magazine at the end of

1896 reveals to us something of the aspirations he had in those early years, and how the Spirit of God was teaching him and preparing him for greater things. This is what he wrote then:

"This year there were no conversions in the villages. There were last year. What is the reason? This reason we are seeking to-day—the two or three workers here and myself. The very thought of seeking has been started and confirmed to-day by mentioning the matter in this letter. We are thinking of taking to-morrow just as a day of prayer for this purpose, and if we do, I believe it will be fruitful. If our hearts and lives are not right, but become right before God, we shall receive a great blessing; or if it be delayed, it will be like holding back a strong-flowing river which will come with mighty power when let go. I believe that if our hearts are right Christ's love *must* give us immediate, constant, unmeasured, ever-increasing blessing. It is the essence of love to be thus. If the heart be right blessing cannot be withheld, it can only be delayed; and to delay such blessing means only that it should overwhelm when it does come.

"Personally, this faith in the love of Christ is a new thought, and it is not the least of the blessings for which I have to be thankful. The life in Christ is a wondrous life—sometimes an experience of joy that can only be described by the words—'*They shall mount up with wings as eagles;'* and how the currents of life sweep upward, too, from the solid rock, as in the thick of flying darts one realises that he stands upon the atonement of Jesus Christ; that, standing on the rock of His death he may claim every promise of the Bible; that is in spite of what we are or feel. *'It is all right.'* I find the nearer one comes to Jesus Christ the more earnestly he prays the 51st Psalm."

In 1897, Mr. Hyde writes: "Had a great privilege last summer in a six weeks' vacation at Poona, near Bombay, in Mr. R. P. Wilder's home. His home is such a holy place, and he is so sensible and happy, too. Our Christians are taking more interest in the work than I have ever known before. God is blessing individuals among us in Bible study, confession of sin, and restitution."

Sickness and Convalescence

In 1898 we find that God was preparing him for work in a very different way. God was answering his prayers and leading him along a path that he would never have chosen for himself. For seven months he was laid aside; he had typhoid fever, and this was followed by two serious abscesses in his back, which caused such nervous depression, that he was compelled to take absolute rest. When convalescent he wrote several short letters, extracts of which follow:

"For a long time after my illness of last May, nervous weakness kept me in the hills, though I wished much to go back to work. I did not leave the hills until December 1st—spent a few days in Ludhiana at our Annual Mission Meeting; then a few days in Lahore, reaching my home (Ferozepore) just before Christmas. All along the year, the prayer of Jabez (1 Chron. 4. 10), was running in my mind. I prayed, 'Enlarge my border,' with perhaps some temporal things much in mind and hope. The answer was an illness, straitening and limiting strength and efforts—taking me, keeping me from work for months, pressing home lessons of waiting, impressing the great lesson, 'Not my will but Thine be done.' But with the waiting and straitening came spiritual enlarging. How often God withholds the temporal, or delays it, that we may long for and seek the spiritual."

"The mission work during the past year has been greatly hampered by lack of funds in the treasury of the Board. The cut of this year was greater than ever before. Perhaps the lack of funds is due to the lack of prayer to Him who says, 'The silver is Mine and the gold is Mine' (Hag. 2. 8). The Indian Church is putting forth great effort for self-support. Our whole Mission unites in prayer every Sunday for the outpouring of the Holy Spirit upon us. Since my return to Ferozepore I have not been very strong, and have spent only two weeks and a half in itinerary work, but these days were greatly blessed. The people listened very attentively and many were turned to Christ. I baptised several, and many more enrolled themselves as catechists. Will you not, each one, seek God's face in prayer for India and for me that my health may be precious in His sight? India is so exhausting, and I do want to stay here."

At the Close of the Year

The letter sent to the College Magazine at the close of the year 1899 shows us very clearly how the Lord was leading Hyde on to the prayer life and into it. The letter we believe will speak to the souls of many of our members. How many of us have trained our bodies to endure the strain and burden of souls? As far back as 1899, Hyde began to accustom himself to "prayer nights." No doubt there are many who have such burdens upon them that they have to spend nights in prayer. Let us ponder over the 1899 letter.

"The years have been full of trial which tells even on physical power, and I have not known how to work below my capacity to withstand and endure. The spiritual things of India have been intense in my soul, and my body is not trained to bear their strain easily. The past year I have been in Ferozepore, and have been well, but just now (March) I am trying to recover somewhat from the strain of the winter. It has been one of work and prayer. Results I have not seen, or but little. There are a few inquirers, and our work has seen a few baptisms. I am a helper of Dr. Newton and his family, and want, as Meyer says, to help my Heavenly Father a little in His work. Have felt led to pray for others this winter as never before. I never before knew what it was *to work all day and then pray all night before God* for another. Early in the morning, 4 or 5 o'clock, or even earlier, and late at night to 12 or 1 o'clock. In College or at parties at home, I used to keep such hours for myself or pleasure, and can I not do as much for God and souls?

"This letter is all about myself, but you will forgive me, I know. May the Lord be with you all."

A Challenge to Service

The word "challenge" has been much in use in religious circles the last two or three years. It is a *challenge* to the Church, a *challenge* to service, a *challenge* to faith, a *challenge* to prayer, etc., and truly these are days of challenge. This is a challenge to us! Are we to go on just preparing the way for the Lord's work? Or are we going forth to reap the harvest? To do this we need to venture more on God. He challenges us to do so! We must be willing to be ridiculed by men; we must be ready to be considered crazy men. The Lord loves nothing more or better than a venture of faith; and when the Lord challenges us are we going to slacken our hands or go forward to win and conquer? "Prove Me now, saith the Lord, if I will not open the windows of Heaven and pour out such a blessing that there will not be room enough to contain it." Most of us are ready to fall in when success begins to come, but the Lord calls for leaders, pioneers in this work, venturing on God.

It is this that strikes us so forcibly in Hyde. He challenged God and God challenged him, and he would take hold of God and would not let Him go, and God would take hold of him and humble him, and make him almost a laughing-stock at one time, hated at another time, but he just clung to God whatever men might say or do, and with what result! Is not this a challenge to us from the Living God to venture all on Him? "To let go" is not easy; "to take the plunge" needs faith; "to continue" in spite of adverse circumstances—these are marks or signs that the challenge has been accepted. To the timid ones the account of Hyde's life during the next few years that we shall record, viz., 1900 and onwards, will be most encouraging.

This is what he said in 1900. "There is an ailment out here called

The 'Punjab Head'

It is not the 'big head,' but a queer head. Having it, one gets over-conscientious, does unwise things, adopts extreme opinions, cannot be guided by others, etc. K—— thinks I have it, and has been lecturing me the past year on the need of being wise. He has told me various things, and since I cannot say he was mistaken, I suppose I must forgive him. I am still at Ferozepore, living in Dr. Newton's home, as for seven years past. It is not a small privilege to be allowed to live in a saintly home."

1901. "The spiritual condition of the Christians in the village this year has reminded me of the Corinthian Church of the First Epistle. But God's grace is powerful. We have used the Word and prayed much and worked earnestly, and several of the evils have been removed. Others seem moving. It makes one believe in a living, present Saviour, to see His people blessed in answer to definite prayer, and inquirers, though only a few, asking to be taught, when our condition is so weak in every way. I wonder how the century has begun with you all. I believe it is to be a time of Pentecostal power, of even a double portion of the Pentecostal Spirit. I interpret God as laying a burden of prayer on souls, pouring out the spirit of grace and supplication, that Christians and the unconverted may look on Him whom they pierced, and mourn in deep conviction of sin. I interpret God as opening a fountain for sin and uncleanness, which means a mighty turning unto Him. The past century seems to me like the days of Jesus' earthly ministry, with its marked evangelisation and wonderful amelioration in the physical well-being of men. The Church's piety and spiritual power, also, of the nineteenth century seem like those of the Christians in our Lord's lifetime. The standard was good, but not up to the level of that of the Apostolic age. We live in the latter age. Can we not have a century besides the first which has the normal life of its own age? I hail in the twentieth century, the blessing of our age restored—a Church holy in life, triumphant in faith, self-sacrificing in service, with one aim, to preach Christ crucified 'unto the uttermost part of the earth.' And if this blessing begins with the deadness in the Church and an eclipse of faith in many, it cannot be worse than in the days just preceding Pentecost. The disciples then were shut up to prayer, and can any one say what would happen now if God's Church should give herself up to this same resource?"

In 1902 Mr. Hyde had

His First Furlough.

We know very little about the work he did at home, but in a letter to his beloved friend and fellow-student, he describes his visit to some relations, and says he cannot travel any more because his money had come to an end. He says that he takes care of himself, and closes with the words, "*I am poor and needy, yet the Lord thinketh upon me.*"

This is how he writes for the College Magazine, which reveals to us the working of his mind at the time, or rather, the working of the Holy Spirit within him and through him.

1902. "The home-coming last spring was one of great pleasure.

The Spiritual Life at Home

and the interest in Foreign Missions is distinctly encouraging. There is an advance, too, in both, which, I believe, we all long for. It is a distinct raising of the accepted standards. And if I might I would say its realisation lies in bringing out the Scripture teaching of the fulness of the Spirit. In this is the power needed. 'Ye shall receive power after that the Holy Ghost is come upon you,' and then indeed shall the Church witness at home and unto the uttermost parts of the earth."

In 1903. No communication was received from Mr. Hyde. In 1904, we have a paragraph which reveals to us something of the condition of the people and of himself. When we remember that this was just before the revival in Wales, and afterwards in

India, we see that it is the dark hour before dawn. The burden placed upon our dear friend, which weighed him down even to weariness, but we realise how the Lord was only preparing him for the great part that he was to take in

The Revival in the Punjab

in the following years.

This is the paragraph. "We need many missionaries and your prayers for labourers, both foreign and Indian. We are here in this district alone, two men and three ladies in 950,000 people. This year has been differing from others to me. For ten years after coming to India, I was 'running,' and did not 'grow weary.' But the past year I have been feeling the drudgery and home-sickness of life here. In the midst of this, to 'keep a-pluggin' away' in patience and sweetness and courage and quiet, strong heart for the work—this I think is the finest quality we may have in Christian service. I do not think Isaiah wrote an ante-climax when he said, 'Rise up with wings as eagles, run and not be weary, walk and not faint.' The last must be the true test and strongest manifestation of the Christian life."

In 1905, there was no message from Hyde to the College Magazine. It was in March, 1905, that the Revival commenced in Assam, and regular accounts of the Spirit's work were sent to the *"Nur Apan,"* the Punjab Christian paper, and we can imagine how Hyde would devour these reports and then give himself to prayer.

In 1906. The only report we have from a letter of Hyde's sister, in which we find that he had been transferred to Ludhiana, and lived in Dr. Wherry's house alone with his servants. He had spent much of his time in the villages, and she says that he had seen some of the Revival that was so manifest in many parts of India, and he realised anew the truth of the verse, "*It is not by might nor by power, but by My Spirit, saith the Lord.*"

Praying Hyde

CONCLUSION

A Challenge to Prayer

CONCLUSION

A Challenge to Prayer

FROM beginning to end the two little volumes have been steeped in prayer, and we know now that hundreds have been praying that men may take up the "challenge" that God is sending them, and to-day we are able to say without any hesitation that God is abundantly answering their prayer. Day by day as the postman brought the letters in and so many of the Lord's children speak of blessing, we could only bow down and praise the Lord for His wonderful goodness, at times we had to shout "Hallelujah," and ask the Lord to use the books more and more. It may be profitable for others to hear of these blessings that have come into the lives of men and women. We purposely withhold the names.

Letters About the Challenge.

One says: "I don't know how to tear myself away from the 'Challenge.' I get away to my knees to read and read and read again and ——! If your *life-work* meant putting that book into the hands of God's children! Think what it means, because through its message numbers of the Lord's children have *at last* been led to put prayer *first*."

Another old prayer warrior writes: "Many thanks for the book. It is the life of a wonderful man, one in a thousand, and it makes us feel that we want to have that passion for intercessory prayer, or that power in prayer which we all so much need.

"The book will do great good. In the hard places, and in hard times, when we are up against things seemingly insurmountable, the thought of 'Praying Hyde' will give courage and keep us on our knees till light comes."

Again, "I have read 'The Challenge' through very slowly and carefully, and have derived much spiritual help. There is much food for thought, and I am certain the reading of it will be blessed to many and a great help in our daily walk in life."

Another writes: "Thank you very much for the two copies of 'Present-day Challenge to Prayer' which I received a week ago. I could not go to sleep that night until I had finished reading the little book. It just gripped me and created within me a longing to know the Lord as Hyde did and to be used unreservedly by Him."

Yet another: "Thanks so much for the book on Mr. Hyde. It is fine, and will I am sure prove a great blessing. It is just what I am needing of late. I shall send for more copies later on which I can pass on to others."

Another very interesting letter from a devoted, hard-working lady missionary: "Thank you for the book about Hyde. I have read it and passed it on to one of our catechists. Will you please send me three more copies, so that I can lend them about among our men who know English. I do wish we would, all of us, learn to pray—Europeans and Indians. The so-called 'impossible' would then be done. But alas! not only is prayer neglected, but those who do pray have generally to pay for it. They are either counted lazy or cranks, just as Hyde was. I wonder why so many of us are so obsessed with work, for most of us, if asked, would say that we believed prayer to be the mightiest power there is. I often think of a remark that an old missionary made to me some time ago, and which I heartily endorse: '*Indians had learned to look on us missionaries as friends, as people who would help them, and as good workers, but they had not yet learned to look on us as men and women of God.*' I feel that if we would only spend more time in His presence, our Indian friends would realise Whose we are and would want to be His themselves."

A very busy medical missionary sends us such a helpful note. His quotation from the late Dr. Maclaren's words has been in our mind since we received his letter, and we know others will try to live up to it. This is what he writes: "Many thanks for sending me a copy of 'A Challenge to Prayer.' The reading of it has done me good, and I shall circulate it. One realises more and more the great need for more prayer and meditation. I have had some good times recently, and I am seeking to live all the time in the consciousness of His presence, in close union and fellowship with the Lord. There is a saying of the late Dr. Maclaren of Manchester. Have you ever heard it? '*We should live each day as if Christ had died yesterday, rose again this morning, and is coming again to-morrow.*'"

This is how one devoted worker in England—an ex-missionary —writes: "I believe the books will be mighty instruments in the hand of God in preparing the Bride and making straight the way for the return of our blessed Lord. I long that all the leaders and teachers at our missions and conventions should get the books into their hands—but I believe that Satan would do much to hinder this, for the books will prove to be mighty levers in the hands of the Lord's children. There are many to whom the books will bring no message, for they need awaking on preliminary points, but to others it is a call from the Holy One."

That experienced watchman on the walls of Zion, Mr. Albert Head, wrote: "The ultimate issue of such a message to the Christian Church and Churches is most timely. Very opportunely do they arrive, for the unsettlement of our own beloved nation as well as the kindred nations throughout Europe—and indeed the world—need the unfolding of God's purposes as set forth in His own precious Word, besides the more mundane word, which each contains as to the prophetic indications enunciated, and the awakening message conveying the warning to take heed, 'for the Coming of the Lord draweth nigh.' That this voice comes from India is very opportune, and should result in a wide-spread awakening and constitute an urgent call to study the Word of God individually and collectively as to when these events may be expected."

To us it is most interesting to note the development in the spiritual life of Hyde, and to find how much like ourselves he was in the early days of his life in India.